World Famous

CROOKS & CON MEN

World Famous

CROOKS & CON MEN

Vikas Khatri

PUSTAK MAHAL®

J-3/16 , Daryaganj, New Delhi-110002
☎ 23276539, 23272783, 23272784 • *Fax:* 011-23260518
E-mail: info@pustakmahal.com • *Website:* www.pustakmahal.com

Sales Centre

- 10-B, Netaji Subhash Marg, Daryaganj, New Delhi-110002
  ☎ 23268292, 23268293, 23279900 • *Fax:* 011-23280567
  E-mail: rapidexdelhi@indiatimes.com
- **Hind Pustak Bhawan**
  6686, Khari Baoli, Delhi-110006
  ☎ 23944314, 23911979

Branches

Bengaluru: ☎ 080-22234025 • *Telefax:* 080-22240209
E-mail: pustak@airtelmail.in • pustak@sancharnet.in
Mumbai: ☎ 022-22010941, 022-22053387
E-mail: rapidex@bom5.vsnl.net.in
Patna: ☎ 0612-3294193 • *Telefax:* 0612-2302719
E-mail: rapidexptn@rediffmail.com
Hyderabad: *Telefax:* 040-24737290
E-mail: pustakmahalhyd@yahoo.co.in

ISBN 978-81-223-1206-5

Edition: 2011

Printed at : Param Offsetters, Okhla, New Delhi-110020

CONTENTS

The Princess from Javasu

On the evening of Thursday, April 3, 1817, a bewildered young stranger appeared at a cobbler's cottage in the village of Almondsbury, Gloucestershire, a few miles from Bristol. She had thick black hair, dark eyes, and wore a black turban. No one could understand the strange language she spoke, but she was obviously tired, indicating by signs that she wanted to sleep. The cobbler's wife didn't know what to do, but thinking her probably a foreign beggar, took her to the Overseer of the Poor, whose job was, in the difficult years after the Napoleonic Wars, to arrest all 'common beggars . . . rogues and vagabonds.' Punishment for such crimes would be prison, the workhouse or even transportation in irons to Australia.

But Mr. Hill, the Overseer, was just as mystified by the girl and decided to take her up to Knole park, a large house above the village, and home of Samuel Worrall, the county Magistrate. Mr. Worrall and his American wife Elizabeth had a Greek manservant who spoke several European languages, and from him Mr. Hill thought he could discover the stranger's origins.

The Overseer brought her, albeit reluctantly, to see the Worralls, but neither they nor their manservant could understand the girl's language. Mrs. Worrall was fascinated by her exotic appearance, but Mr. Worrall was more suspicious, asking her by signs if she had any papers with her. The girl emptied out her pockets, but all she had were a few halfpennies and a bad sixpence. Although possessing counterfeit money could mean the death sentence, the girl seemed not to understand the seriousness of the offence. The only other thing she had in her possession was a bar of soap pinned inside a piece of linen. Worrall then asked to look at the girl's hands. They were soft, showing no signs of hard work, and her fingernails were clean and well cared for.

The Worralls thought it best for the stranger to stay the night at an inn in the village, and sent her there accompanied by two of their servants.

Whilst at the inn, the girl noticed a print of a pineapple on the wall and pointed to it enthusiastically, pronouncing 'Anana', indicating that it was a fruit of her homeland. 'Ananas' is the word for pineapple in Greek and many other European languages. The landlady offered to cook the girl supper, but she made it understood that she would rather have tea, which she drank only after repeating a prayer while holding one hand over her eyes. Before drinking a second cup, she insisted on washing the cup herself, and again went through the same ritual as before. The landlady and her little daughter were fascinated. More was to follow. When shown her bed for the night the stranger appeared not to understand its function, instead she lay down on the floor to sleep. It was not until the landlady's daughter showed her how comfortable it was that, after kneeling to say her prayers, she lay on the bed to sleep.

Determined to find out something about the girl, Mrs. Worrall brought her back to Knole to stay. She soon learned that girl's name was 'Caraboo', and that she had come to England in a ship. Caraboo was particularly impressed by various pieces of furniture showing Chinese figures. Perhaps China was her original homeland? There was only one problem that she was entirely European in appearance. Whilst at Knole she behaved oddly, declining all meat and eating only vegetables and drinking only water. But Mr. Worrall and his Greek manservant were still suspicious, so the Magistrate decided to take her to the Mayor in Bristol to be tried, which could mean serious trouble, especially as she'd been found in possession of illegal tender, the dud sixpence.

But John Haythorne, the Mayor, could get nothing intelligible from the girl except the name, Caraboo, and so followed the law for such cases and sent her to St. Peter's Hospital, whilst further enquiries were made.

The Girl's Story

At the overcrowded, dirty hospital she declined all kinds of food and even refused to sleep on the beds. Fascinated gentlemen brought various foreigners who tried to decipher her language, but none was successful.

After a week at the hospital Mrs. Worrall again intervened and took her to stay at her husband's offices in Bristol, where she remained for ten days in the care of her husband's housekeeper. Again troops of foreigners and supposed language experts were brought in to see her without result until, at last, there was some progress. This was in the form of a Portuguese traveller named Manuel Eynesso (or Enes), who said he understood what Caraboo was saying. After a conversation with the girl in her own peculiar language, he told Mr. Worrall her story.

She was a princess from an island called Javasu, who'd been abducted from her homeland by pirates and taken on a long, difficult journey, which ended in her escaping by jumping overboard in the Bristol Channel and swimming to the shore. Eynesso's story was enough to convince Worrall and he brought the newly discovered foreign princess back to Knole immediately.

During her time at Knole the princess delighted the Worralls and their visitors with her idiosyncratic behaviour. She fenced and used a homemade bow and arrow with great skill, danced exotically, swam naked in the lake when she was alone, and prayed to her supreme being 'Allah Tallah' from treetops; all the while maintaining her unusual eating and drinking habits and strange language. Every week more and more gentlemen and ladies poured in to see the exotic lost princess. Caraboo duly responded to the attention with increasingly exotic behaviour and elaborate language, and also provided the full, dramatic narrative of her abduction by pirates from her native Javasu. She now also agreed to write down examples of her language, an example of which was sent to Oxford for analysis. It was returned soon after marked as 'humbug'. Undaunted, the princess had her portrait painted and made herself an elaborate 'traditional' eastern costume, using materials of her choice provided by Mrs. Worrall.

The Unmasking

By now newspapers were full of descriptions of 'Princess Caraboo' and she had become a national figure. But this notoriety was to prove her undoing.

A Mrs. Neale, who ran a lodging house in Bristol, read the description of the princess in the *Bristol Journal* and recognised her immediately. A couple of months earlier the girl had been a lodger at a house which she kept with her daughters, and she'd sometimes entertained them by speaking in her own made-up language. When she left the house she'd been wearing a turban.

The shocked Mrs. Worrall confronted Caraboo with this information obtained from a wheelwright's son who'd called at Knole. He said he'd met the 'princess' on the road two days before she appeared in Almondsbury, and swore she'd eaten steak and drunk rum with him at a public house. Under the weight of such testimony the princess eventually broke down and admitted the truth. She was Mary Baker (born Willcocks), the daughter of a cobbler in Witheridge, Devon.

After the initial disbelief at such an imposture, especially for the kindly, and a little naive Mrs. Worrall, the main question was what was to be done with the girl. She would be an embarrassment to the Worralls if she were allowed to remain in Bristol. It was soon decided to send her to America, where she would be conveniently out of the way.

Mary sailed for Philadelphia on Sunday, June 28, 1817, in the company of three strictly religious ladies whom Mrs. Worrall had asked to take care of her. When she arrived in America, she was greeted by enthusiastic crowds as 'Princess Caraboo', and she gave performances as the princess while there. But she was not always well received, and all traces of her are lost after the first few months. Nothing is known about Mary in America after November 1817, when she wrote her last known letter to Mrs. Worrall.

She seems to have returned to England in 1824, where she exhibited herself as Princess Caraboo in New Bond Street, London, and later in Bristol and Bath. Apparently she was not successful. She travelled in France and Spain for a while after this, but returned to England to marry and settle down in Bristol, where she had a daughter in 1829. She made a decent living selling leeches to Bristol Infirmary Hospital, until she died on Christmas Eve, 1864, aged 75, of a probable heart attack. She was buried in the Hebron Road Burial Ground, Bedminster, Bristol, and lies there still, in an unmarked grave.

The question remains – how had this uneducated country girl managed to fool so many people, some of them highly intelligent academics, for so long, and perhaps more importantly, why? Mrs. Worrall asked the editor of *Felix Farley's Bristol Journal,* John Matthew Gutch, to find out something of the girl's past from Mary herself, and from anyone else he could find who knew or had known her. What Gutch found out is perhaps even more interesting than Mary's couple of months fooling people into thinking she was a foreign princess, and was published as a book in August that year (*Caraboo: A Narrative of a Singular Imposition),* selling very well.

Her parents were interviewed and corroborated some, but not all, of her own romanticised story of her early life. Her father said that she always found it difficult to settle down, and every spring and autumn she grew restless. He thought her not quite right in the head, and attributed this to her contracting rheumatic fever at the age of fifteen, which was when, he said, all the trouble started.

Mary's History

Mary Baker, as she called herself, was twenty-six years old and had born in 1791 into a very poor family where six of her brothers and sisters had died young. From the age of eight she was spinning wool and weaving, and occasionally working on local farms. Later she worked as a maid in a house in Exeter, but walked out after eight weeks because the work was too hard. She went back home to Witheridge, but found life there unbearable after her taste of the outside world, and ran away after a week.

On the road to Taunton, Mary said she had attempted to hang herself from a tree by her apron strings, but heard a voice in her head telling her it was a sin. She then met a man on the road who felt sorry for her and gave her enough money for three night's lodgings in Taunton.

After Taunton she went to Bristol, begging along the way, then decided to walk to London. She got within thirty miles of the city before collapsing, to be given a lift by a waggoner with two other women as far as Hyde Park Corner. She again collapsed, and the two women, realising she was very ill, took her to St. Giles' Workhouse Hospital, where she was admitted to the fever ward. She was given boiling hot baths and had the back of her head 'cupped' in a painful operation without anesthetic, which involved cutting the skin in several places and applying hot glasses to draw the blood out, supposedly to alleviate the fever. She stayed several months before she was taken into the care of a Presbyterian clergyman called Pattenden, who took a liking to her though he found her 'odd and eccentric'.

Mr. Pattenden found Mary a job with a Mr. and Mrs. Matthews, looking after their children. Here she became good friends with the cook of a Jewish family who lived next door, and developed an interest in their prayers, diet, and the Hebrew alphabet, which would come in useful when she assumed the role of Princess Caraboo four years later. She also learned to read and write while she was there, and wrote letters home to her family. She made up imaginative stories and games for the children and all seemed to be going well. Then, in April 1812, she suddenly left.

For some reason she spent four days at St. Mary's Workhouse, and then went back. The Matthews liked her, but found her behaviour mysterious and eccentric; she sometimes told them she would like to go and live wild in the woods.

In the Autumn of 1812 she left the Matthews house for good after an argument. She wanted to go abroad and persuaded a friend, a Mrs. Baynes, to write a letter to her parents saying that she'd 'left England with a travelling family.' But in reality, in February 1813, she applied to the Magdalen Hospital for reformed prostitutes under the name of Ann Burgess, Burgess being her mother's maiden name. She told Gutch and others that she mistook the place for a nunnery, but this was pure fantasy. At first she told the Magdalen Committee that she'd been seduced by a gentleman staying at a house she'd worked at in Devon. He'd taken her to London, she said, but abandoned her after a month. After this she 'went on the town' leading a loose life. She was accepted and given work as a housemaid. But a few weeks later she admitted that she'd never been a prostitute, her name was not Burgess, and she'd just needed somewhere to stay. The officials asked her about her living relations, her father was dead, she told him, and if they asked her any more about her family she would hang herself.

The records of Magdalen Hospital show her to have been well behaved during her stay, though 'very eccentric', and given to depression and restlessness. This latter was particularly true, and she left the hospital in July.

According to Mary's story, the next thing she did was to set off back home to Witheridge, disguised as a man because of the dangers of walking across Hounslow Heath alone. She then crossed Salisbury Plain where, according to her, she was kidnapped by highwaymen who took her back to their camp. When they discovered she was a girl they were ready to shoot her as a police spy, but she begged for her life and was released.

She eventually arrived home in Autumn 1813. Her mother found her a job working for a leatherworker and tanner in Crediton, a few miles from her village. She left after three months, objecting to having to carry the hides.

After a couple of other jobs she again headed back to London, where she worked for a fishmonger in Billingsgate. Mary claimed that while working here, in Spring 1814, she had a love affair with a gentleman called Baker. After two months they were married and lived together for a while in London and possibly at Battle, near Hastings. Then her husband sent her back to London, while he sailed to Calais, promising to bring her over to France. But that was the last she ever heard from him. Whether any of this was true remains open to question, but when Mary returned to London at the beginning of 1816, she was pregnant. She managed to get a job working behind the bar in a pub run by a Mrs. Clark, where she called herself Hannah and developed a reputation for telling strange stories.

The baby was born on February 11, 1816; but where it remains a mystery. He was christened John Wilcox, but Mary called him John Edward Francis Baker. As there was no father present for support and Mary had no money, both were sent to St. Mary's Workhouse on 19th April, where they stayed until the 17th June. Here she was persuaded to give the child to the Foundling Hospital. But to do this she had to give references, personal details; something she was never happy doing; and say why she could not support the child herself. The few prosaic facts she subsequently provided are probably as close to the truth as she ever came. She gave her name as Mary Willcocks, said she was unmarried, aged 25, and that the father of the child was John Baker, a bricklayer from Exeter. In a more detailed statement given later at the hospital, she said they'd lived together for nine months in Exeter before walking to London, where he deserted her.

After she left the hospital Mary found employment again, and visited the child at the Foundling Hospital every Monday, until, on the 27th of October 1816, he died. At this time, she was working for a family called Starling, and Mrs. Starling remembered her telling them that the child had died at her mother's house. She also said that Mary was an excellent servant but 'out of her mind'. She described her behaviour as eccentric and unusual, always telling the children frightening stories about gypsies, and that she'd been born in the East Indies and the baby was born in Philadelphia. She was eventually sacked in November for setting fire to the beds.

She may have spent Christmas 1816 in France, but she returned to Devon in February 1817 by coach. Coach travel was expensive, so she must have had money from somewhere. She told her parents that the baby had died and she was coming to say goodbye before she sailed for the Indies. After ten days at home she sent her trunk on ahead, and set out for Bristol to leave for the Indies. But rather than going north to Bristol, she ended up begging on the road to Plymouth, and according to her account, staying with gypsies. She left them and headed back through Exeter to Bristol, where she arrived on 10th March.

She was now looking for a ship to take her to Philadelphia, and found she could travel steerage on one leaving in fifteen days, for five guineas, which she would have to try and raise. She found lodgings sharing a room with a young Jewish girl called Eleanor, in a respectable house belonging to a Mrs. Neale. The two girls went out begging in the streets together during the day. Apparently, after noticing the attention that French lace-makers from Normandy received wearing high lace headdresses, Eleanor persuaded Mary to use her black shawl as a turban to make her look more interesting.

They tried this for a while, but Mary was restless again and left Bristol, still pretending to be French and using her own made-up language, begging at various places along the road to Gloucester. This disguise proved successful until she met someone who could speak French, but she quickly improvised and claimed to be Spanish. It was now that she met the wheelwright's son who helped to expose her later. She spoke to him and various other people they met on the road in her strange language, and they were all eager to help her. When she arrived at a pub speaking her lingo, the landlady asked her in for a drink and soon the whole pub was offering her food and drink, but she refused.

She got away and headed back on road towards Clifton, still accompanied by the wheelwright's son. Soon after, they met two men, one of whom said he spoke perfect Spanish, so Mary was forced to speak to him in her language, which, amazingly he claimed to understand as Spanish, 'translating' what she said and saying that her mother and father were following her along the road. For Mary this was an important lesson in how to use other people's 'expertise'.

By now Mary was tired of the wheelwright's son, and after letting him buy her a steak and a cup of tea at a pub on the way into Bristol, managed to lose him on the quay. She stayed the night in lodgings and the next morning started out on the road to Gloucester, once again assuming her character as she headed towards the village of Almondsbury, and fame as Princess Caraboo.

How did she do it?

Mary Willcocks was not the first imposter to fool high society, but she was one of the most successful. How had she managed to maintain the hoax? The crucial factor seems to have been people's belief that she could not understand or read English. Once they convinced themselves of this, they had no scruples about what they said in front of her, providing much of the information she needed for her role with their conversations and the books they showed her describing exotic places and languages. As many who knew her noted, she had a remarkable memory.

So, as Mary gathered more detailed information from the various learned visitors to Knole, particularly those who wanted to show off their knowledge, her role became more substantial and her behaviour more convincingly princess-like. She was also surrounded by people, Mrs. Worrall in particular, who desperately wanted to believe she was a foreign princess. She was fulfilling a need for the romance of unseen lands in people's lives. Maybe she had been to France and picked up some French and Spanish, it certainly seems that she spent some time with the gypsies, as she used some gypsy words as part of her lingo. But these were just the trimmings, the main part of her character was developed at Knole park.

And what of the mysterious Portuguese traveller Manuel Eynesso? How had he understood and 'translated' her language if she'd made it up? Was he an accomplice? A lover? The father of her child? He was certainly used by Mary to cement her identity. We'll probably never know the truth, perhaps he was just another hoaxer trying his luck at breaking into high society, as Mary Willcocks had done so successfully.

Sarah Wilson – The Princess Susanna Hoax

Sarah Wilson was born in a Staffordshire village in 1754, the daughter of a bailiff. She left for London when she was just sixteen, and after only a few weeks in the city had the fortune to be employed as a maid to Miss Caroline Vernon, a lady-in-waiting to Queen Charlotte. Miss Vernon seems to have admired her intelligence and conscientiousness.

At the 'Queen's House' (where Buckingham Palace now stands) she saw Queen Charlotte, wife of King George III, frequently and learned much about private royal affairs and life at Court. But soon this quick-witted girl began to grow envious of all the wealth and finery surrounding her.

One day, when alone in the Queen's closet, she broke open the cabinet and stole some jewellery, a miniature portrait of the Queen, and one of the Queen's dresses. Perhaps she thought such relatively minor theft would go undetected, but the Queen was in the habit of counting her most valuable pieces and noticed some were missing. She had the closet watched to find the culprit. A few days later Sarah again went to steal from the same place, but this time she was caught in the act. She was charged with theft and violation of the royal privacy, and sentenced to death.

But after Caroline Vernon's pleas to the Queen on Sarah's behalf, the punishment was commuted to transportation and, in July 1771, at the age of seventeen, Sarah was taken by prison ship to Baltimore, Maryland.

On arrival in America, she was sold to a Mr. W. Devall of Bush Creek, Frederick County, but she escaped to Virginia almost immediately.

Somehow, she still had amongst her personal belongings some of the stolen items from the Queen; including a ring, a dress, and the miniature portrait. Now the imposture began to take shape. She transformed herself into 'Princess Susanna Caroline Matilda, sister of Queen Charlotte', forced into exile in America following a scandal and a family quarrel.

With her intimate familiarity with Court life and her knowledge of the gossip of upper class English society, 'Princess Susanna' was soon in demand at various gentlemen's houses. She particularly impressed those of the older generation of settlers who were emigrants from England themselves, as they listened, fascinated, to her stories of the old country. Some had other motives; as people not unreasonably assumed, the princess would soon be restored to favour back in England, so in return for favours to be granted when she regained her rightful position, she was often given money and gifts.

The imposture was proving a success, although some were suspicious about her refusal to speak German, despite being born in the country, and her perfect grasp of the English language. There were also those who wondered why they had never heard of a younger sister of the Queen before.

Meanwhile, Sarah's former owner, Mr. Devall, who'd paid a considerable sum for her, had been trying hard to find his escaped slave, and eventually came to hear about this travelling 'princess'. He knew from the description that it was Sarah Wilson. So, in the Autumn of 1773, he circulated an advertisement saying that the supposed princess was in fact his escaped servant girl, and that whoever caught her would receive five pistols and all expenses as a reward. He also sent one of his employees, Michael Dalton, to find her.

Dalton tracked her down to a plantation in Charlestown, but she had left before he arrived; he eventually found her on a neighbouring plantation and brought her back to slavery in Bush Creek at gunpoint.

This seemed to be the end of the story, and for a while Sarah worked without incident for Devall. But after two years, she found the opportunity she'd been waiting for to plan her escape. Another slave girl named Sarah Wilson had recently arrived in Maryland, and she utilised this coincidence and a further piece of good luck, Devall's departure to fight in the militia in the American War of Independence, to the full. Somehow she was able to exchange the new Sarah Wilson for herself, and escaped northward out of slavery once and for all.

This time Devall gave up the chase.

She later married William Talbot, a young officer in the Light Dragoons. After the war the couple stayed in America, possibly because she would have been arrested again if she returned to England. Sarah used the money earned from her role as Princess Susanna to set her husband up in business. Her wandering days over, they subsequently had a large family and lived in the then respectable area of the Bowery, New York.

The Faker Famous for his 'Sexton Blakes'

Brilliant faker Tom Keating rocked the art world he despised with his amazing imitations of the works of great masters. In 1979, at the age of sixty-two, he went on trial at the Old Bailey for forgery. But all the charges were dropped when his health deteriorated.

Keating, a big bearded ex-naval stoker, called his fakes, in Cockney rhyming slang, 'Sexton Blakes'. At first he painted them to get even with the dealers who had, he reckoned, exploited him.

As a young man, he had lived in a damp prefab with his wife and two children, and was paid £5 a time to copy other artists. He angrily quit the job when he found his paintings on sale in galleries for £500.

'Those dealers are just East End blokes in West End suits,' he said. 'They don't give a damn about the paintings. All they're after is the profit.'

In the 1950s his marriage broke up and he went to Scotland to restore murals. While he was there he began imitating the works of other painters and sending them to auction.

He returned to London in 1960 for his most important commission – restoring the pictures in Marlborough House which had been empty since the death of Queen Mary in 1953.

One day, he met Queen Elizabeth while carrying out the restoration of a giant painting by Laguerre of the Duke of Marlborough.

In his book, The Fake's Progress, Keating recalls: 'The Queen came up the stairs and gazed at it in astonishment. She turned to me and mentioned that she had run up and down the stairs hundreds of times as a little girl but had not been aware these beautiful pictures were on the wall. "Well they are madam," I said. "And there's a lot more under the black varnish on the other walls."'

Then, according to Keating, the Queen watched him use a solvent to clean a section of the painting.

The work at Marlborough House was an isolated job for hard up Keating. Most of his time would be spent turning out his 'Sexton Blakes' by the score, giving most of them away but selling others through auction rooms.

In 1963, he read a book on the 19th-century artist Samuel Palmer and became captivated by him. He scoured the art galleries looking for examples of Palmer's work to copy. At the Tate, said Keating, he touched one 'and a strange sensation went through me like an electric shock'.

Keating was a perfectionist. He was always careful about selecting the right paper or canvas. And he claimed that the spirit of Palmer would guide his hand.

'I'd sit in my little sketching room waiting for it to happen,' he explained. 'I have never drawn a sheep from life but then Palmer's sheep would begin to appear on the paper. Then

Palmer's Valley of Vision Watched Over by the Good Shepherd in the Shadow of Shoreham Church. With Sam's permission, I sometimes signed them with his own name, but they were his, not mine. It was his hand that guided the pen.'

It was also in 1963 that Keating met Jane Kelly, a pretty convent educated schoolgirl busy studying for her exams. In Bohemian coffee bars, she and her friends would cluster round the painter, treating him almost as a guru.

Jane was seventeen, Keating fourty-six. Yet, after the death of her boyfriend in a road accident, they fell in love – and the impressionable teenager became the painter's mistress. They moved to historic Wattisfield Hall in Suffolk, where Jane restored pictures and Keating embarked on a prodigious output of fakes.

When, at the Old Bailey in 1979, Keating was shown his most famous fake – a sepia, ink wash of Sepham Barn sold for £9,400 as a genuine Palmer – he told the jury: 'I am ashamed of this piece of work.'

He had no recollection of painting it, he said. It had, however, been done using modern materials, the main figure of a shepherd was 'un-Palmerish' and the flock of sheep 'unsheep-like'. It was the sort of painting, he confessed, that he would normally have burnt or thrown away.

Looking at another work subsequently sold for £2,550, Keating appeared bemused and said: 'That must have taken me about half an hour. It's just a doodle. It has the ingredients of Palmer but not his technical ability of aesthetic appeal'.

The 'doodle' was of a barn at Shoreham, which had been sold at a country auction for £35. It was later sold by a London gallery to Bedford Museum for £2,550 after restoration work by the National Gallery.

After the sale of Sepham Barn, Keating and Jane went to live in Tenerife. There, Jane met a Canadian with whom she fell in love and whom she later married. The nine-year affair between Jane and Keating was over. They met again seven years later – when Jane gave evidence at the Old Bailey about Keating's famous fakes. The scandal, which ruined many reputations in the art world, broke after an expert had written in *The Times* suggesting Sepham Barn was not genuine.

By Keating's own rough count, no fewer than 2,500 of his fake pictures are hanging in galleries or on collectors' walls. No one will ever know which fakes are and which are old masters. Not even Tom Keating who, after his trial was stopped, continued turning out his paintings – at a price.

Because of his notoriety, Keating's works became highly priced. 'Suddenly everyone wants to own a Keating,' said one gallery owner. 'Prices have doubled in a month. His paintings are going round the world.'

Keating was offered a £250,000 contract from one London gallery and a £30,000 commission for a single portrait. He turned both down.

'I have enough work to make me rich beyond my wildest dreams,' he said. 'But I've met many millionaires and they have all been miserable. All I have ever wanted to do is to paint. I would give all the damn things away if I could afford to. Painting is God's gift, not mine, and it should be used to bring pleasure.'

At the height of his fame, a television film was made about the master-faker's life and work. Director Rex Bloomstein got to know him well. He said of Keating:

'He was a very emotional man. When painting, he would cry and shiver. He said he felt the artist come down and guide his hand. He was the most fascinating, and complex person I have ever met.'

The Man who Cheated the World

The first class passengers on the liner *Ile de France*—bound for Southampton and Cherbourg—were intrigued by the sallow-faced "mystery man" who occupied the largest and most luxurious stateroom. It was noted that all his meals were brought to his quarters . . . that a tough-looking bodyguard or detective patrolled the corridor outside the cabin . . . that the millionaire (for surely he must be one) only came out after dark — when he went to the deserted shooting range and practised with a revolver.

Occasionally he was seen strolling on deck around midnight. But if anyone came near him or attempted to speak, he would turn and disappear into the fog that crawled in from the Atlantic and shrouded the ship. Long before the *Ile de France* reached England, rumours had the man down as a gangster on the run, a wealthy maniac on his way to a Swiss sanatorium, or a film star wearing an impenetrable disguise—a wig that made him look almost totally bald, a black tie, dark suit, walking stick and diamond tiepin.

The truth, however, was stranger (and sadder) than any of the speculations made in the dining room and bars during that voyage in March 1932.

The man was Ivan Kreuger, the Swedish Match King, master forger, and self-styled "Saviour of Europe". He was returning from New York—where he had unsuccessfully tried to raise £13 m to pay the interest on several outstanding bank loans—to appear before a special committee set up by the Swedish government to investigate his complicated and multifarious business concerns.

Despite his international interests and reputation, few people had seen the fifty-two-year-old tycoon in the not very attractive flesh. Known to his few intimates as "The Quiet One", Kreuger loathed having his photograph taken and refused to grant newspaper interviews.

"Devourer of Men"

One journalist who did get to meet him wrote: "This is no human being, but a reptile with sunk in and stinging eyes. He is a devourer of men!" Instead of feeling insulted Kreuger was flattered by the description—which, he said, reminded him of his idol, Napoleon.

But Kreuger, faced with economic ruin and personal disgrace, was not the man of steel the business world supposed him to be. When the crunch came he snapped as easily as one of the millions of matchsticks he had manufactured and sold. As the *Ile de France* prepared to dock at Southampton he summoned the man in the corridor—a detective named John C. Brown—into his stateroom.

Brown had been employed by the American banker J. P. Morgan, to ensure that Kreuger did not attempt to take his own life—as he had threatened do in Wall Street a few days earlier. Morgan thought that Kreuger—who owed him $11 m over a phoney telephone deal, might jump overboard in mid-Atlantic. "He's not the sort to do it with razor or a gun," Morgan stated. "He likes a touch of the mysterious. 'Kreuger Vanishes at Sea' is more to his taste than 'Kreuger Shoots Himself!'"

Once in Kreuger's presence the private detective was appalled by the panic and terror in the financier's face. He had been on the verge of a nervous breakdown in New York, when he had answered telephones that hadn't rung, shouted for nonexistent callers to enter his room, and issued urgent orders only to cancel or contradict them minutes later.

Now, Kreuger was reduced to wheedling, craven wreck. With hands and voice shaking he whispered: "You know that my American and worldwide credits are falling due." The detective nodded. "And that my Italian Treasury Bills—worth

$ 60 m — are said to be forged." Again Brown inclined his head. "Then you must save me . . . help me get away . . . let me escape."

"I know that. Mr. Morgan knows that. And soon the whole world will know it," Brown exclaimed. "It's too late to help you now—even if I could."

Tears welled in Kreuger's bloodshot eyes and his sensual lips quivered. "I'll give you all the money you ever dreamed of. A million dollars—a million pounds. Anything—just name it!"

Brown turned away from him and walked to the door. "What do you propose paying me in, Mr. Kreuger," he asked as he left. "Forged bonds?"

With one bluff called. Kreuger would have been justified in returning to Stockholm and surrendering himself to Swedish justice. For years he had cheated the world by means of issuing forged shares, debenture certificates and securities; by borrowing money from one country to lend to another and not repaying the original debt; by faking balance sheets and bank statements; by mortgaging assets several times over; by preparing false contracts and forging the signatures on them.

Double dealing

As his network of double dealing and deceit grew bigger and more intricate, Kreuger refused to tell his co-directors of the Swedish Match Trust—the foundation of his empire—more than a chapter of the full financial story. With the passing of the years his nerves and memory failed him.

He could no longer remember whom he had borrowed money from and which merger had gone through or failed.

"I will gain control by foul means, or fair if I have to," he told his colleagues cynically. "Do not ask to see my books. There are none—except for those I keep in my head."

It was this attitude of contempt and indifference to ethics that made him gamble on one last piece of audacity. He cabled his Paris office from the *Ile de France* and arranged a meeting in the capital on Friday, March 11, with Kristen Littorin, his oldest friend and trusted second-in-command.

If Littorin was unable to help him out of the mess then he knew what he would do. Until then there was his revolver skill to perfect, and letters to write to those who had admired and stood by him from his early days when he had trained in his father's match factory at Kalmar, in southern Sweden.

The safety match had been invented in Sweden in 1848—thirty-two years before Ivar Kreuger was born—but at the beginning of his career, he had little time for such "a commonplace, unexciting object".

Leaving the factory, he studied to be a mechanical engineer and then emigrated to America, where for a time he earned his living as a salesman and a railway linesman. Later, he worked as an engineer in Mexico and in 1908 returned to Sweden and set up his own construction company which built the country's first steel-reinforced concrete skyscraper. By 1913, however, his interest had swung back to matches. With the increase in cigarette smoking, and the growing popularity of pipes and cigars, he realised that the "silly little bits of wood" were not to be despised after all.

Also, he discovered that it was possible to raise the price of the cheaply produced matches, and reduce the number of matchsticks in a box, without anyone noticing or complaining too much.

"After all," he pointed out. "Whoever bothers to count the number of matches in a box—and to discover if there are 50 in it or only 46?"

Rivals Gobbled Up

Within two years he had gained control of seven factories and then he founded the mighty Swedish Match Trust, which quickly gobbled up rival match firms throughout Sweden and Europe. At the age of fourty he was the undisputed Match King and his Match Palace in Stockholm rivalled that of any genuine royalty.

It was an impressive 125-room block which an American journalist described in hushed prose. "The moment you pass the finely wrought iron gates," he wrote. "You get the atmosphere of some continental palace. Instead of the dusty, tarnished splendour of a departed day, however, it is bright and gleaming. Massive marble columns surround what the French call a court of honour. In the center is a bronze fountain surmounted by a graceful, poised figure of Diana . . ."

Kreuger's study and second floor office had a symbolic torch over the door and a bust of Napoleon on the antique desk. The suite—which included a soundproofed "Quiet Room"—was furnished and panelled in dark, "restful" oak.

On a side table Kreuger had a battery of telephones, one of which rang whenever his foot pressed a button on the floor. To impress a particularly important visitor he would pick up the bogus instrument and conduct a long and intimate "conversation" with the Italian dictator Mussolini, or one of the crowned heads of Europe.

Boast of Mistresses

Due to his strange appearance Kreuger found it difficult—if not impossible—to win the affections of women without resorting to payment or bribes. Many people in Stockholm thought him to be homosexual, but in fact he had a varied succession of prostitutes who spent the night with him in his superb maisonette flat at 13 Villagaten.

The industrialist had town houses, city apartments and country mansions in a dozen different countries, and, he boasted a mistress in "every civilised capital". These liaisons were kept from the press and the public, and if the women in question were married then their husbands were silenced with money.

It was not until Kreuger's death that–his chief mistress, or courtesan, Ingaborg Hassler, wrote and published her memoirs. She first met Kreuger in the early 1920's when she was only seventeen years old, and for the next six years she pestered him for marriage.

"If you will not marry me I will marry another man," she threatened. "Go ahead," Kreuger told her. "It's my money you're interested in—not me. Anyway you will be back within six months."

Half a year later she left her second choice husband and returned to Kreuger, who rewarded her with pearls and diamond. "Never have I met a man who cajole you as he did," she wrote. "He had a remarkable talent for being persuasive." But other girls, presumably less well rewarded than Ingaborg, spoke scathingly of Kreuger as a man and a lover. "He was mean with his emotions and mean with his money," one of them told a Stockholm journalist. "He was what you call a rabbit!"

Meanwhile, on the financial scene, Kreuger continued to expand his interests until, by 1924, he controlled nearly 70 percent of the world's match production. He used his millions, so he claimed, to help countries which were in economic difficulties and which would "go under without me".

In 1925 he let it be known that he had advanced $12 m to Spain, and had in his possession a document signed by the Spanish Prime Minister on behalf of King Alfonso, guaranteeing him 16 percent interest a year. Later that year, he boasted of a similar fictitious arrangement with Poland—and then proceeded to borrow money from French and American banks on the strength of the forged and worthless contracts.

"Mind you, not a word of this to the Stock Exchange or the Bourse," he would caution. "If anything was leaked then it would mean the end of Spain, the fall of Poland. In fact, it would probably bring about war!"

These preposterous statements were accepted by bankers who would normally have thought twice before giving a penny to a beggar in the streets. But Kreuger, with his silver tongue and golden assurances, succeeded in borrowing untold millions of kroner from them. It was only after the Wall Street crash in October 1929, and the Great Depression that followed, that the banking houses demanded to see the colour and substance of his assets.

By the winter of 1931, when he sailed to America, stayed at his ten room apartment in Park Avenue, and tried to raise 13 m from J. P. Morgan, he knew that he could no longer defend himself by words alone. Morgan's curt dismissal of him, and his bizarre voyage on the *Ile de France*, had prepared him for the end. What genuine securities and actual cash he possessed he made over to his brother, Torsten. He bought farewell presents for his secretary and housekeeper in Stockholm.

Then, on March 11, 1932, he went to meet Krister Littorin and some associates in the Hotel Meurice in Paris. The businessmen and bankers assembled in an upstairs room, and Kreuger pleaded for further credit, another outsize loan. The financiers heard him out—then Littorin put the one question to Kreuger that could save him or send him under.

"lvar," said his friend gently. "Tell us about the $60 m you have in Italian Treasury Bills. They might be used to put you in the clear."

Mussolini Secret

Kreuger stared blankly at him for a moment. "Oh those," he said vaguely. "I got them from Mussolini. He gave them to me as payment for a secret loan."

Littorin shrugged his shoulders and sighed. "But I've already spoken with Mussolini," he chided. "He knows nothing about the bills. He says he discussed such a loan with you twice—in 1927 and 1930—but you couldn't come to terms. He also says that if you have any bills they must be forged. Is that true?'"

Kreuger raised his head. "No," he lied. "It is not true. The bills are genuine."

Shortly after that the meeting broke up. Kreuger said goodbye to Littorin and walked to a gunmaker's shop near his flat in the Avenue Victor Emmanuel. He bought a nine millimeter revolver, a hundred cartridges, and retired for the night. The following afternoon, when Kreuger failed to turn up for a further meeting, Littorin hurried to his boss's third floor apartment.

There, lying fully dressed on the silk sheets, was the body of Ivar Kreuger. A revolver lay on the floor by the bed, and there was a bullet in the center of the tycoon's heart. Before the gun had fallen from his fingers he had held it so close to his chest that his shirt and waistcoat were scorched around the bullet hole.

Littorin backed pale-faced to the door, and at seven o'clock that night the news of Kreuger's suicide was being flashed throughout the world. The repercussions to his death were swift and dramatic. At midnight on Sunday, March 13, the Swedish Parliament hastily assembled to discuss how they could best stabilise the krone when the Paris Bourse and the London and New York Stock Exchanges opened the next day.

In Estonia, the head of the Kreugar-controlled State Match Company shot himself behind locked doors. In Paris, the French Premier, Andre Tardieu, conferred at length with the Swedish ambassador. In Switzerland, the Bank for International Settlement, which had been brought into being by Kreuger—held a emergency meeting.

But it was not until March 14 that the main panic occurred. Then shares companies owned, controlled or even inspired by the dead financier dropped to rock bottom. Hundreds of people who had never seen or met Ivan Kreuge found themselves out of work or in danger of dismissal.

Economic Shock

It took weeks for the situation to right itself. And although Sweden survived the economic shock, her prestige and goodwill suffered badly. "The world knows us through only two people—Kreuger and Garbo," moaned a leading Stockholm businessman. "Now we only have Garbo left—and she threatens to retire!"

Kreuger knew that a slump was inevitable. But in a farewell note to Littorin he stated that whatever he did, or did not do, his country and its people would be the losers. "I have made such a mess of things," he wrote, "that I believe this to be the most satisfactory solution for all concerned . . . Goodbye now and thanks. I.K."

✿✿

King of the Gypsies

Bampfylde Moore Carew was born in July 1693, in Bickleigh, near Tiverton in Devon, less than twenty miles from Witheridge, the birthplace of Mary Willcocks, alias Princess Caraboo. He was the son of the reverend Theodore Carew, the Carews being an ancient local family, and his godfathers at his baptism were Hugh Bampfylde and a Major Moore, hence his name. At the age of twelve Carew was sent to Tiverton and progressed well in his first four years there, excelling in Latin and Greek, and also less scholarly pursuits, especially hunting with his school friends.

Soon his attention was taken up entirely by hunting, and on one occasion – while chasing a deer through fields of ripening corn his hunting party caused a great deal of damage to the crops. Complaints were made to the headmaster by the affected farmers and Carew and his schoolmates were so severely threatened about what might become of them that they ran away from school. They eventually found themselves at an alehouse just outside Tiverton where they fell in with a group of gypsies and spent the night drinking with them. Impressed by the freedom these people enjoyed, Carew and his companions decided to join their numbers there and then. This agreement meant following the gypsy's particular laws and form of government, and paying allegiance to an elected gypsy king.

Through his actions and buoyant personality it wasn't long before Carew became notorious and respected among the gypsies, mainly for his skill in disguise and trickery. Outside the gypsy fraternity, amongst the more gullible, he had a local reputation as an astrologer and fortune teller. On one occasion he was consulted by a certain Madam Musgrove who suspected that there was a large amount of money buried somewhere around her house, and promised a large reward if he located it. Carew pretended to study his 'secret art' and told the lady that the treasure lay under a laurel tree in her garden, but she should delay the search until her planet of good fortune was in the right position. The lady was delighted and rewarded Carew with twenty guineas. Of course, when the poor woman finally decided to dig beneath the laurel tree she found nothing there.

Bampfylde Moore Carew.
King of the Beggars.

After a year and a half of gypsy living, Carew returned home to his parents but grew bored with home life and left once more to join the gypsies. Over the next few years using various ingenious disguises, such as a lunatic called 'Mad Tom', a seaman, a zealous clergyman, a rat catcher, and even an old woman, he extracted money from various gentlemen throughout the West Country, some of whom knew him well but were apparently unable to see through his disguises. He later eloped with the daughter of a respectable apothecary and was subsequently married at Bath, then travelled with his wife to Bristol and through Somerset, Dorset and Hampshire. In Gosport they paid a visit to Carew's uncle who offered him money to quit the gypsy life and return to his family – Carew refused – he was having much fun.

Clause Patch, the king of the gypsies, lay dying and a vast number of gypsies descended on London to choose a new king. Carew was duly elected 'King of the Mendicants (beggars)'. There followed more disguises – often that of a shipwrecked sailor looking for alms – and scams until he was captured at Barnstaple in Devon. He was moved to Exeter where he was imprisoned for two months and then brought up for trial loaded with chains at the quarter sessions at Exeter castle. Being asked by the judge which countries he had travelled in, Carew answered – Denmark, Sweden, Russia, France, Spain, Portugal, Canada and Ireland, proving that he had imagination at least. The judge answered that he must prepare himself for a hotter climate as he was to be transported as a convict to Maryland.

After an eleven week voyage the prison ship arrived at its destination and all one hundred prisoners were ordered to tidy themselves up for sale the next day. The planters arrived next morning to view the slaves and while a group of them were arguing over his purchase Carew managed to escape into the woods. He was recaptured, whipped for his trouble and like Henry More Smith fitted with a heavy iron collar. He escaped again, and concealing himself in the day and travelling only by night eventually met with a tribe of friendly Indians who released him from the neck iron. He left them and travelled through Pennsylvania in the guise of a Quaker and subsequently as a sailor conning money out of wealthy merchants using various tall stories.

He made his way to New York, at that time a city of around seven thousand inhabitants, and got passage on a boat sailing to Bristol. But wary of rearrest in England, he pricked his hands and face with the point of a dagger, rubbed them in salt and gunpowder and groaned in agony to convince those who tried to arrest him that he was suffering from smallpox.

Again he travelled around the West Country extracting money by begging, usually disguised as a shipwrecked seaman, and at Maiden Bradley in Wiltshire met an even more desperate looking beggar than himself. They joined company and begged together through the town and at the house of Lord Weymouth, a local noble well-known for his severe treatment of impostors. It took some time for Carew to find out that his ragged companion was actually Lord Weymouth himself – disguised as he often was to gauge the response and attitudes of local residents to such beggars.

Some time after this, with Carew in disguise as a decrepit old man selling matches and collecting old rags, he met another ragman and they arrived together at a place called Gutter-Hall in Porlock, north Devon. Here they found no lodgings but were told of a house they could stay in for free with food thrown in, they soon found out why – the house was haunted. The local farmer asked the two beggars to lay the ghost of an old woman who haunted the place, if they were successful the reward would be twenty shillings. They stayed the night there accompanied by the farmer's solidly-built son, whom they scared out of his wits by throwing handfuls of stones down the stairs. Next morning they reassured the farmer that they had laid the ghost and received their reward. Apparently, the house was quiet after this.

On one occasion, whilst out walking in Exeter, Carew was recognised, captured and forced without trial into a ship sailing once again to Maryland. During the sixteen week journey the captain died and Carew himself was infected with fever. On arrival in Maryland Carew again escaped, this time in a canoe, and made for the woods. He travelled by night to avoid his pursuers and hid in trees by day, stealing food from houses and farms when he could. According to his own account he crossed the River Delaware on horseback before arriving at Rhode Island and thence to Boston, estimating the population then at twenty-four thousand and comparing a beacon hill there, where pulleys drew up a lighted barrel of tar to warn the country in case of invasion, to Glastonbury Tor.

Back home, he was again reunited with his wife and daughter. Visiting a relation of his, Sir Thomas Carew, the gypsy king was again offered a comfortable living if he would forsake his vagabond way of life. Again he refused.

In 1745, curious about news of the Jacobite rebellion under Bonnie Prince Charlie (or the Young Pretender as he was known), he travelled north to Edinburgh, there meeting up with the rebels. Because of his apparent enthusiasm for their cause he was asked to join their number, but feigned illness and lameness and was excused. Nevertheless, he apparently travelled among the rebels south to Carlisle and on to Manchester and then Derby, where he heard a report that the Duke of Cumberland was coming to fight them. Lack of support from English Jacobites and French allies persuaded the rebels to withdraw to Carlisle, though Bonnie Prince Charlie himself was against this. After the withdrawal, Carew headed homewards being careful to change his note to 'God bless King George, and the brave Duke William!'

Once more reunited with his wife, he began to feel too old for his former exertions and devoted himself to revising the laws of the gypsy community, but a serious illness forced him to resign his kingship and spend his last years in his hometown of Brickleigh. One story goes that he came into some money on the death of a relative, another through winning a lottery, and bought a house in the country. He lived to see his daughter's marriage and grandchildren, and died around 1758. He is buried in the local churchyard at Brickleigh.

Carew seems to have been the consummate 18th century rogue and vagabond, though his stories also suggest real ingenuity in matters of disguise and trickery – making him a sort of Frank Abagnale of the 1700s. The first account of his life – *The Life and Adventures of Bampfylde-Moore Carew* – was published in 1745, whilst he was still living. Unfortunately it's not known how much of the book is fact, as alternative reliable sources for his escapades are extremely limited. However, it is clear he was a nationally renowned figure, he was mentioned in contemporary magazines, and is even referred to in the popular literature of the day, such as Thackeray's *Vanity Fair*. In the West Country, he was a local hero and known throughout the region as 'King Carew'.

✿✿

The Man who Sold Eiffel Tower

Victor Lustig was a con artist who undertook scams in various countries and became best known as "*The man who sold the Eiffel Tower, Twice.*"

Victor Lustig was born in Hostinne, Czech Republic, but soon headed to The West. He was a glib and charming con man, fluent in multiple languages. He established himself by working scams on the ocean liners steaming between Paris and New York City.

One of Lustig's trademark cons involved a "money-printing machine". He would demonstrate the capability of the small box to clients, all the while lamenting that it took the device six hours to copy a $100 bill. The client, sensing huge profits, would buy the machines for a high price, usually over $30,000. Over the next twelve hours, the machine would produce two more $100 bills. After that, it produced only blank paper, as its supply of $100 bills became exhausted. By the time the clients realised that they had been scammed, Lustig was long gone.

Eiffel Tower Scam

In 1925, France had recovered from World War I, and Paris was booming, an excellent environment for a con artist. Lustig's master con came to him one spring day when he was reading a newspaper. An article discussed the problems the city was having maintaining the Eiffel Tower. Even keeping it painted was an expensive chore, and the tower was becoming somewhat run down. Lustig saw the possibilities behind this article and developed a remarkable scheme.

Lustig had a forger produce fake government stationery for him and invited six scrap metal dealers to a confidential meeting at the Hotel de Crillon, one of the most prestigious of the old Paris hotels, to discuss a possible business deal. All six

attended the meeting. There, Lustig introduced himself as the deputy director-general of the Ministry of Posts and Telegraphs. He explained that they had been selected on the basis of their good reputations as honest businessmen, and then dropped his bombshell.

Lustig told the group that the upkeep on the Eiffel Tower was so outrageous that the city could not maintain it any longer, and wanted to sell it for scrap. Due to the certain public outcry, he went on, the matter was to be kept secret until all the details were thought out. Lustig said that he had been given the responsibility to select the dealer to carry out the task. The idea was not as implausible in 1925 as it would be today. The Eiffel Tower had been built for the 1889 Paris Exposition, and was not intended to be permanent. It was to have been taken down in 1909 and moved somewhere else. It did not fit with the city's other great monuments like the Gothic cathedrals or the Arc de Triomphe, and at the time, it really was in poor condition.

Lustig took the men to the tower in a rented limousine for an inspection tour. It gave Lustig the opportunity to gauge which of them was the most enthusiastic and gullible. Lustig asked for bids to be submitted the next day, and reminded them that the matter was a state secret. In reality, Lustig already knew he would accept the bid from one dealer, Andre Poisson (coincidentally, in French the word *poisson*, which means "fish" in English, is also used as a derogatory epithet for someone who is particularly gullible). Poisson was insecure, feeling he was not in the inner circles of the Parisian business community, and thought that obtaining the Eiffel Tower deal would put him in the big league.

However, Poisson's wife was suspicious, wondering who this official was, why everything was so secret, and why everything was being done so quickly. To deal with her suspicion, Lustig arranged another meeting, and then "confessed". As a government minister, Lustig said, he did not make enough money to pursue the lifestyle he enjoyed, and needed to find ways to supplement his income. This meant that his dealings needed a certain discretion. Poisson understood immediately. He was dealing with another corrupt government official who wanted a bribe. That put Poisson's mind at rest immediately, since he was familiar with the type and had no problems dealing with such people.

So Lustig not only received the funds for the Eiffel Tower, he also collected a large bribe. Lustig and his personal secretary, a Franco American con man Robert Arthur Tourbillon also known as Dan Collins, hastily took a train for Vienna with a suitcase full of cash.

Surprisingly, nothing happened. Poisson was too humiliated to complain to the police. A month later, Lustig returned to Paris, selected six more scrap dealers, and tried to sell the Tower once more. This time, the chosen victim went to the police before Lustig could close the deal, but Lustig and Collins managed to evade arrest.

Later Years

Later, Lustig convinced Al Capone to invest $50,000 in a stock deal. Lustig kept Capone's money in a safe deposit box for two months, then returned it to him, claiming that the deal had fallen through. Impressed with Lustig's integrity, Capone gave him $5,000. It was, of course, all that Lustig was after.

There were others who made a profit selling civic landmarks. In the early 1920s, a rival to Lustig could have been the fast-talking Scotsman Arthur Furguson, but his very existence is questioned.

In 1930, Lustig went into partnership with a middle-aged chemist from Nebraska named Tom Shaw. Shaw had the job of engraving plates for the manufacture of counterfeit banknotes. They then organised a counterfeit ring for the purpose of circulating the hundreds of thousands of forged notes throughout the country. Lustig was successful in keeping it a secret by making sure that not even the underlings knew anything about it.

On the evening of May 10, 1935, Lustig was arrested by federal agents on charges of counterfeiting after an anonymous phone call was made, out of jealousy, by his mistress Billy May, who became jealous when she learned of the romance between him and Shaw's young mistress Marie. The day before his trial, he managed to escape from the Federal House of Detention in New York City, but was recaptured 27 days later in Pittsburgh. Lustig pleaded guilty at his trial and was sentenced to twenty years in Alcatraz Island, California. On March 9, 1947, he contracted pneumonia and died two days later at the Medical Center for Federal Prisoners in Springfield, Missouri. On his death certificate, his name is listed as Robert V. Miller and his occupation was listed as "apprentice salesman."

Ten Commandments

A set of instructions known as the "Ten Commandments for Con Men" has been widely attributed to Lustig:

- ✔ Be a patient listener (it is this, not fast talking, that gets a con man his coups).
- ✔ Never look bored.
- ✔ Wait for the other person to reveal any political opinions, then agree with them.
- ✔ Let the other person reveal religious views, then have the same ones.
- ✔ Hint at sex talk, but don't follow it up unless the other person shows a strong interest.

- ✔ Never discuss illness, unless some special concern is shown.
- ✔ Never pry into a person's personal circumstances (they'll tell you all eventually).
- ✔ Never boast – just let your importance be quietly obvious.
- ✔ Never be untidy.
- ✔ Never get drunk.

✿✿

The Pitfalls of Literature

Two of the most famous forgers of all time were teenagers. Both lived in the 18th century, both forged literature, and their names were Thomas Chatterton and William Henry Ireland.

Chatterton became known as 'the Marvellous Boy'. Before he was ten he had taught himself how to write in Gothic characters by copying from an old Bible. In 1765, when only twelve, he started producing ancient poems which he claimed he had found in an old chest in the local church. He said they had been written by a priest named Thomas Rowley, possibly around Chaucer's time – 400 years earlier.

Not only did these odes convince scholars of their antiquity but they also received some fine critical acclaim. Spurred by his success, Thomas left his native Bristol for London. But the London experts were not fooled so easily and declared his works to be forgeries.

Although he had a minor success with his own poems and political satires, Thomas Chatterton's career was soon in ruins and at seventeen he took his own life.

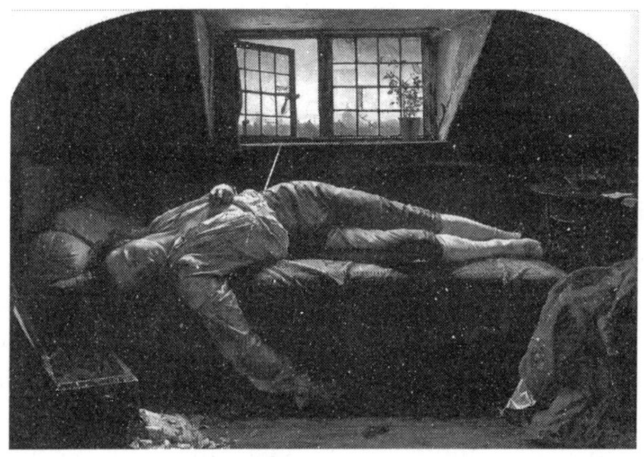

In his will, he left 'all the young ladies my letters and poems. I leave my mother and sister to the protection of my friends if I have any.'

Chatterton was later recognised to have been a budding genius. He became an inspiration to later poets such as Wordsworth, Shelley and Coleridge. He was immortalised in a painting by Henry Wallis and is the only forger to have had an entire opera written about him – Leoncavallo's Chatterton.

The other teenage forger of that time was William Henry Ireland who, although not so talented, also made the stage – with a Shakespearian production which he wrote himself.

William had started early by handing over spurious Shakespearian manuscripts and artefacts to his father, a London bookseller and Shakespeare enthusiast. William claimed that while working as a solicitor's clerk, a mysterious gentleman had entrusted all the documents into his safekeeping. These he showed his father, who showed them to friends – and the news of the Shakespeare discoveries spread like wildfire.

What began as a jape rapidly turned into an industry. The young Ireland produced a land deed and other private papers of

William Shakespeare. Then he got bolder and produced original transcripts of parts of King Lear and extracts from Hamlet. These were so convincing that even the diarist and biographer James Boswell paid homage. He said: 'I now kiss the invaluable relics of our bard to thank God that I have lived to see them.'

With this sort of success under his belt, Ireland really went to town. At the age of seventeen, he 'discovered' a brand new Shakespearean play which no one had seen before. He called it Vortigern.

The play was produced at the Drury Lane Theatre on April 2, 1796. The actor-manager John Kemble, who was to play the lead, had his doubts about the authenticity of the piece and suggested that it would have been more appropriate to open the play a day earlier on April Fool's Day. But although the play did open on April 2, Kemble got the last laugh. In Act Five there was a speech which contained a line that brought the house down. . . .

'And when this solemn mockery is ended. . . .'

The audience hooted the rest of the play off the stage. The first performance of Vortigern was also its last and the game was up for Ireland. The rest of his forgeries were detected and the teenager confessed to everything — although his old father could never bring himself to believe that his treasured possessions were all fakes.

Ponzi Schemes

Charles Ponzi was an Italian swindler, who is considered one of the greatest swindlers in American history. His aliases include Charles Ponei, Charles P. Bianchi, Carl and Carlo. The term "Ponzi scheme" was coined because of Charles Ponzi's scam and today it is the description of any scam that pays early investors returns from the investments of later investors. Charles Ponzi promised clients a 50% profit within 45 days, or 100% profit within 90 days, by buying discounted postal reply coupons in other countries and redeeming them at face value in the United States as a form of arbitrage. Ponzi was probably inspired by the scheme of William F. Miller, a Brooklyn bookkeeper who in 1899 used the same scheme to take in $1 million.

Early Life

Parts of Charles Ponzi's life are somewhat difficult to determine, owing to his propensity to fabricate and embellish facts. He was born Carlo Pietro Giovanni Guglielmo Tebaldo Ponzi in Lugo, Italy in 1882. He told *The New York Times* that he had come from a well-to-do family in Parma, Italy. He took a job as a postal worker early on, but was soon accepted into the University of Rome La Sapienza. His friends considered the university a "four-year vacation," and he was inclined to follow them around to bars, cafés, and the opera.

Arrival in America

On November 15, 1903, he arrived in Boston aboard the S.S. *Vancouver*. By his own account, Ponzi had $2.50 in his pocket, having gambled away the rest of his lifesavings during the voyage. "I landed in this country with $2.50 in cash and $1 million in hopes, and those hopes never left me," he later told *The New York Times*. He quickly learned English and spent the next few years doing odd jobs along the East Coast, eventually taking a job as a dishwasher in a restaurant, where he slept on the floor. He managed to work his way up to the position of waiter, but was fired for shortchanging the customers and theft.

In 1907, Ponzi moved to Montreal and became an assistant teller in the newly opened *Banco Zarossi*, a bank started by Luigi "Louis" Zarossi to service the influx of Italian immigrants arriving in the city. Zarossi paid 6% interest on bank deposits – double the going rate at the time – and was growing rapidly as a result. He eventually rose to bank manager. However, Ponzi found out that the bank was in serious financial trouble because of bad real estate loans, and that Zarossi was funding the interest payments not through profit on investments, but by using money deposited in newly opened accounts. The bank eventually failed and Zarossi fled to Mexico with a large portion of the bank's money.

Ponzi stayed in Montreal and, for some time, lived at Zarossi's house helping the man's abandoned family, while planning to return to the United States and start over. As Ponzi was penniless, this proved to be very difficult. Eventually he walked into the offices of a former Zarossi customer *Canadian Warehousing* and, finding no one there, wrote himself a check for $423.58 in a chequebook he found, forging the signature of a director of the company, Damien Fournier. Confronted by police who had taken note of his large expenditures just after the forged cheque was cashed, Ponzi held out his hands wrist up and said "I'm guilty." He ended up spending three years in the prison *St. Vincent-de-Paul* near Montreal. Rather than inform his mother of this development, he posted her a letter stating that he had found a job as a "special assistant" to a prison warden.

After his release in 1911 he decided to return to the United States, but got involved in a scheme to smuggle Italian illegal immigrants across the border. He was caught and spent two years in Atlanta Prison. Here he became a translator for the warden, who was intercepting letters from mobster Ignazio "Lupo the Wolf" Saietta. Ponzi ended up befriending Lupo. However, it was another prisoner who became a true role model to Ponzi—Charles W. Morse. Morse, a wealthy Wall Street businessman and speculator, fooled doctors during medical exams, poisoning himself by eating soap shavings, toxins that left his body as quickly as the doctors left his bedside. Morse was soon released from prison. Ponzi completed his prison term the summer following Morse's release, having an additional month added to his term due to his inability to pay a $500 fine.

Origin of the term "Ponzi Scheme"

When Ponzi was released from prison, he eventually made his way back to Boston. There he met Rose Maria Gnecco, a stenographer, whom he asked to marry. Though Ponzi did not tell Gnecco about his years in jail, his mother sent Gnecco a letter telling her of Ponzi's past. Nonetheless, she married him in 1918. For the next few months, he worked at a number of businesses, including his father-in-law's grocery, before hitting upon an idea to sell advertising in a large business listing to be sent to various businesses. Ponzi was unable to sell this idea to businesses, and his company failed soon after.

A few weeks later, Ponzi received a letter in the mail from a company in Spain asking about the catalogue. Inside the envelope was an International reply coupon (IRC), something which he had never seen before. He asked about it and found a weakness in the system which would, in theory, allow him to make money.

The purpose of the postal reply coupon was to allow someone in one country to send it to a correspondent in another country, who could use it to pay the postage of a reply. IRCs were priced at the cost of postage in the country of purchase, but could be exchanged for stamps to cover the cost of postage in the country where redeemed; if these values were different, there was a potential profit. Inflation after World War I had greatly decreased the cost of postage in Italy expressed in U.S. dollars, so that an IRC could be bought cheaply in Italy and exchanged for U.S. stamps of higher value, which could then be sold. Ponzi claimed that the net profit on these transactions, after expenses and exchange rates, was in excess of 400%. This was a form of arbitrage, or profiting by buying an asset at a lower price in one market and immediately selling it in a market where the price is higher, which is not illegal.

Seeing an opportunity, Ponzi quit his translator's job to set his scheme in motion. He borrowed money and sent it back to his relatives in Italy with instructions to buy postal coupons and send them to him. However, when he tried to redeem them, he ran into an avalanche of red tape.

Undaunted, Ponzi went to several of his friends in Boston and promised that he would double their investment in 90 days. The great returns available from postal reply coupons, he explained to them, made such incredible profits easy. Some people invested and were paid off as promised, receiving $750 interest on initial investments of $1,250.

Soon afterward, Ponzi started his own company, the "Securities Exchange Company," to promote the scheme. He set up shop in a building on School Street. Word spread, and investments came in at an ever-increasing rate. Ponzi hired agents and paid them generous commissions for every dollar they brought in. By February 1920, Ponzi's total take was US $5,000, (approximately US $54,000 in 2008 dollars). By March, he had made $30,000 ($328,000 in 2008 terms). A frenzy was building, and Ponzi began to hire agents to take in money from all over New England and New Jersey. At that time, investors were being paid impressive rates, encouraging yet others to invest. By May 1920, he had made $420,000 ($4.59 million in 2008 terms).

He began depositing the money in the Hanover Trust Bank of Boston (a small bank on Hanover Street in the mostly

Italian North End), in the hope that once his account was large enough he could impose his will on the bank or even be made its president; he did, in fact, buy a controlling interest in the bank (through himself and several friends) after depositing $3 million. By July 1920, he had made millions. People were mortgaging their homes and investing their lifesavings. Most did not take their profits, but reinvested.

Ponzi was bringing in cash at a fantastic rate, but the simplest financial analysis would have shown that the operation was running at a large loss. As long as money kept flowing in, existing investors could be paid with the new money. In fact, new money was the only way Ponzi had to pay off those investors, as he made no effort to generate legitimate profits.

Ponzi lived luxuriously, he bought a mansion in Lexington, Massachusetts, with air conditioning and a heated swimming pool, and he maintained accounts in several banks across New England besides Hanover Trust. He also brought his mother from Italy in a first class stateroom on an ocean liner. She died soon afterward.

Suspicion

Ponzi's rapid rise naturally drew suspicion. However, when a Boston financial writer suggested there was no way Ponzi could legally deliver such high returns in a short period of time, Ponzi sued for libel and won $500,000 in damages. As libel law in those days placed the burden of proof on the writer and the paper, this effectively neutralised any serious probes into his dealings for some time.

Nonetheless, there were still signs of his eventual ruin. Joseph Daniels, a Boston furniture dealer who had given Ponzi furniture which he could not afford to pay for, sued Ponzi to cash in on the gold rush. The lawsuit was unsuccessful, but it did start people asking how Ponzi could have gone from being penniless to being a millionaire in so short a time. There was a run on the Securities Exchange Company, as some investors decided to pull out. Ponzi paid them and the run stopped. On

July 24, 1920, the *Boston Post* printed a favourable article on Ponzi and his scheme that brought in investors faster than ever. At that time, Ponzi was making $250,000 a day. Ponzi's good fortune was increased by the fact that just below this favourable article, which seemed to imply that Ponzi was indeed returning 50% return on investment after only 45 days, was a bank advertisement that stated that the bank was paying 5% returns annually. The next business day after this article was published, Ponzi arrived at his office to find thousands of Bostonians waiting to give him their money.

Despite this reprieve, *Post's* acting publisher Richard Grozier and city editor Eddie Dunn were suspicious and assigned investigative reporters to check Ponzi out. He was also under investigation by the Commonwealth of Massachusetts, and on the day the *Post* printed its article, Ponzi met with state officials. He managed to divert the officials from checking his books by offering to stop taking money during the investigation, a fortunate choice, as proper records were not being kept. Ponzi's offer temporarily calmed the suspicions of the state officials.

Collapse of the scheme

By this time, Ponzi was seeking another deal to get him out of trouble, but time was running out. On July 26, the *Post* started a series of articles that asked hard questions about the operation of Ponzi's money machine. The *Post* contacted Clarence Barron, the financial analyst who published the *Barron's* financial paper, to examine Ponzi's scheme. Barron observed that though Ponzi was offering fantastic returns on investments, Ponzi himself was not investing with his own company.

Barron then noted that to cover the investments made with the Securities Exchange Company, 160 million postal reply coupons would have to be in circulation. However, only about 27,000 actually were. The United States Post Office stated that postal reply coupons were not being bought in quantity at home or abroad. The gross profit margin in percent on buying and selling each IRC was colossal, but the overhead required to handle the purchase and redemption of these items, which were of extremely low cost and were sold individually, would have exceeded the gross profit.

The stories caused a panic run on the Securities Exchange Company. Ponzi paid out $2 million in three days to a wild crowd outside his office. He canvassed the crowd, passed out coffee and donuts, and cheerfully told them they had nothing to worry about. Many changed their minds and left their money with him. However, this attracted the attention of Daniel Gallagher, the United States Attorney for the District of Massachusetts. Gallagher commissioned Edwin Pride to audit the Securities Exchange Company's books—an effort made difficult by the fact his bookkeeping system consisted merely of index cards with investors' names.

In the meantime, Ponzi had hired a publicity agent, William McMasters. However, McMasters quickly became suspicious of Ponzi's endless talk of postal reply coupons, as well as the ongoing investigation against him. He later described Ponzi as a "financial idiot" who did not seem to know how to add.

The denouement for Ponzi began in late July, when McMasters found several highly incriminating documents that indicated Ponzi was merely robbing Peter to pay Paul. He went to his former employer, the *Post*, with this information. The paper offered him $5,000 for his story. On August 2, 1920, McMasters wrote an article for the *Post* declaring Ponzi hopelessly insolvent. The article claimed that while Ponzi claimed $7 million in liquid funds, he was actually at least $2 million in debt. With interest factored in, McMasters wrote, 'Ponzi was as much as $4.5 million in the red.' The story touched off a massive run, and Ponzi paid off in one day. He then sped up plans to build a massive conglomerate that would engage in banking and import-export operations.

However, trouble came from an unexpected quarter—Massachusetts Bank Commissioner Joseph Allen. An initial investigation into Ponzi's banking practices found nothing illegal, but Allen was afraid that if massive withdrawals exhausted Ponzi's reserves, it would bring Boston's banking system to its knees. When Allen found out a large number of Ponzi-controlled accounts had received more than $250,000 in loans, he ordered two bank examiners to keep an eye on Ponzi's accounts. On August 9, they reported that enough investors had cashed their cheques on Ponzi's main account that it was almost certainly overdrawn. Allen then ordered Hanover Trust not to pay out anymore cheques from Ponzi's main account. He also orchestrated an involuntary bankruptcy filing by several small Ponzi investors. The move forced Massachusetts Attorney General J. Weston Allen to release a statement that there was little to support Ponzi's claims of large-scale dealings in postal coupons. State officials then invited Ponzi note holders to come to the Massachusetts State House to furnish their names and addresses for the purpose of the investigation. On the same day, Ponzi received a preview of Pride's audit, which revealed Ponzi was at least $7 million in debt.

On August 11, it all came crashing down for Ponzi. First, the *Post* came out with a front page story about his activities in Montreal thirteen years earlier—including his forgery conviction and his role at Zarossi's scandal-ridden bank. That afternoon, Bank Commissioner Allen seized Hanover Trust after finding numerous irregularities in its books. Although the commissioner did not know it, this move foiled Ponzi's last-ditch plan to "borrow" funds from the bank vaults after other efforts to obtain funds failed.

With reports that he was due to be arrested any day, Ponzi surrendered to federal authorities on August 12 and was charged with mail fraud for sending letters to his marks telling them their notes had matured. He was originally released on $25,000 bail, but after the *Post* released the results of the audit, the bail bondsman withdrew the bail due to concerns he might be a flight risk.

The news brought down five other banks in addition to Hanover Trust. His investors were practically wiped out, receiving less than 30 cents on the dollar. The *Post* won a Pulitzer Prize in 1921 for its exposure of Ponzi's fraud.

Prison and later life

In two federal indictments, Ponzi was charged with 86 counts of mail fraud. At the urging of his wife, on November 1, 1920, Ponzi pleaded guilty to a single count before Judge Clarence Hale, who declared before sentencing, "Here was a man with all the duties of seeking large money. He concocted a scheme which, on his counsel's admission, did defraud men and women. It will not do to have the world understand that such a scheme as that can be carried out . . . without receiving substantial punishment." He was sentenced to five years in federal prison.

He was released after three and a half years and was almost immediately indicted on 22 Massachusetts state charges of larceny. This came as a surprise to Ponzi; he thought he had a deal calling for the state to drop any charges against him if he pleaded guilty to the federal charges. He sued, claiming that as a federal prisoner he could not be tried by the state. The case, *Ponzi v. Fessenden*, made it all the way to the Supreme Court. On the 27th of March, 1922, the Supreme Court ruled that plea bargains on federal charges have no standing regarding state charges. It also ruled that Ponzi was not facing double jeopardy because Massachusetts was charging him with larceny while the federal government charged him with mail fraud (even though the charges implicated the same criminal operation).

In October 1922, he was tried on the first ten larceny counts. Since he was insolvent, Ponzi served as his own attorney and, being as persuasive as he had been to investors, the jury found him not guilty on all charges. He was tried a second time on five of the remaining charges, and the jury deadlocked. Ponzi was found guilty at a third trial, and was sentenced to an additional seven to nine years in prison as "a common and notorious thief."

After word got out that Ponzi had never obtained American citizenship (despite having lived in the United States for most of the time since 1903), federal officials initiated efforts to have him deported as an undesirable alien in 1922.

Ponzi was released on bail as he appealed the state conviction. He went to the Springfield neighbourhood of Jacksonville,

Florida and launched the Charpon Land Syndicate ("Charpon" is an amalgam of his name), offering investors in September 1925 tiny tracts of land, some under water, and promising 200 percent returns in 60 days. In reality, it was a scam that sold swampland in Columbia County. Ponzi was indicted by a Duval County grand jury in February 1926 and charged with violating Florida trust and securities laws. A jury found him guilty on the securities charges, and the judge sentenced him to a year in the Florida State Prison. Ponzi appealed his conviction and was freed after posting a $1,500 bond.

Ponzi travelled to Tampa, where he shaved his head, grew a moustache, and tried to flee the country as a crewman on a merchant ship bound for Italy. The ship, however, made one last American port call; he was caught in New Orleans and sent back to Massachusetts to serve out his prison term. Ponzi served seven more years in prison.

In the meantime, government investigators tried to trace Ponzi's convoluted accounts to figure out how much money he had taken and where it had gone. They never managed to untangle it and could conclude only that millions had gone through his hands.

Ponzi was released in 1934. With the release came an immediate order to have him deported to Italy. He asked for a full pardon from Governor Joseph B. Ely. However, on July 13, Ely turned the appeal down. His charismatic confidence had faded, and when he left the prison gates, he was met by an angry crowd. He told reporters before he left, "I went looking for trouble, and I found it."

Rose stayed behind and later divorced him in 1937, as she did not want to leave Boston. Rose, who later remarried, eventually became the bookkeeper for the New Cocoanut Grove Inc, the parent company of Boston's Cocoanut Grove Nightclub.

In Italy, Ponzi jumped from scheme to scheme, but little came of them. He eventually got a job in Brazil as an agent for Ala Littoria, the Italian state airline. During World War II, however, Brazil sided with the Allies, and the airline's operation in the country was shut down. During that time, Ponzi also wrote his autobiography.

Death

Ponzi spent the last years of his life in poverty, working occasionally as a translator. His health suffered. A heart attack in 1941 left him considerably weakened. His eyesight began failing, and by 1948, he was almost completely blind. A brain hemorrhage paralysed his right leg and arm. He died in a charity hospital in Rio de Janeiro, the Hospital São Francisco de Assis of Federal University of Rio de Janeiro on January 18, 1949.

Supported by his last and only friend who spoke English and had notions of Italian, the barber Francisco Nonato Nunes, Mr. Ponzi granted one last interview to an American reporter, telling him, "Even if they never got anything for it, it was cheap at that price. Without malice aforethought I had given them the best show that was ever staged in their territory since the landing of the Pilgrims! It was easily worth fifteen million bucks to watch me put the thing over." He also admitted, after years of maintaining his innocence, that he had engaged in a swindle.

The Most Wanted Men in the West

What was the truth about the Wild West? Our ideas tend to have been formed by characters like Tom Mix, Gene Autry, the Lone Ranger and Roy Rogers. Screen idols through the years have portrayed the cowboy as a slick, good-looking, gun-totin', lariat twirling goodie in a white hat, or scheming, scowling baddie in a black hat.

Hollywood took the names of men like Billy the Kid, Jesse James and Butch Cassidy and turned them into heroes. But few of the folk who lived and died in the 19th century West would have agreed. . . .

Jesse James

Baptist minister's son Jesse Woodson James strolled into the Clay County Savings Bank in Liberty, Missouri, on February 13, 1866, and took the liberty of relieving cashier Mr. Greenup Bird of $60,000.

It was the start of a bloodthirsty war that the James boys and their daring cousins, the Youngers, waged throughout Kansas and Missouri. They got away with gunning down train guards and bank tellers because nobody knew what the villains looked like – since none of them ever had his photograph taken.

Jesse would openly stroll around Nashville and Kansas City, calling himself Mr. Howard, and on one occasion even bought a drink for a Pinkerton Agency detective searching for him.

Detective Bligh confided to 'Mr. Howard' that his last wish would be to confront Jesse James. Later James sent him a note: 'Go ahead and die. You've seen Jesse James.'

Jesse loved playing to the crowd. On one occasion during a Missouri train holdup, he personally presented the guard with his latest press cuttings.

The day Jesse and his boys slipped up was when they tried to rob the First National Bank in Northfield, Minnesota. The townsfolk had been tipped off that the gang were on their way, and as they arrived in town they were met with a hail of bullets, grapeshot and even bricks. Two of the gang were blown to pieces, three Younger brothers were captured, but Jesse got away.

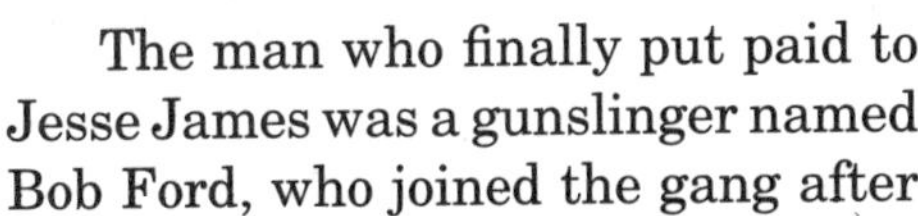

The man who finally put paid to Jesse James was a gunslinger named Bob Ford, who joined the gang after secretly agreeing with the authorities to assassinate James for a free pardon and part of the reward money.

On April 3, 1882, Jesse, then aged thirty-five, got up to straighten his favourite 'Home, Sweet Home' picture on the wall of his bunkhouse abode. Ford blew off the back of his head, and his brains scattered across the floor.

The owner of the house where Jesse died, at St Joseph, Missouri, chopped up the floor and sold the bloodstained wood-shavings for five dollars a time.

Cole Younger

The James gang's greatest partners in crime were the Younger family. Cole Younger, then twenty-eight, first teamed up with Jesse's gang in Logan County, Kentucky, in 1868, to rob the local bank.

Cole had already met Jesse as one of Quantrill's Raiders at the massacre of Lawrence, Kansas, where, in one of the most unparalleled acts of savagery in the West, 150 men and boys were shot by William Quantrill's Confederate guerillas.

Cole had a passionate love affair with Myra Belle Shirley, the eighteen-year-old daughter of a Dallas horse breeder. After two disastrous marriages, she went on to achieve notoriety as Belle Starr.

The other Younger brothers – Bob, eighteen, Jim, twenty-six, and John, twenty-eight – later joined Cole in the James gang. John died from a Pinkerton bullet and the surviving three were captured and jailed for life after the Northfield, Missouri shootout.

Butch Cassidy

Butch Cassidy and the Sundance Kid were turned into posthumous superstars thanks to one successful film. In real life, neither were heroes – although a cut above some of the other crooks of the age.

Butch Cassidy was born in 1867 in Beaver, Utah, and was named Robert Leroy Parker, but later changed his name as a token of respect to his idol Mike Cassidy who taught him the arts of rustling and horse stealing.

In his youth, Butch was involved in everything from petty larceny to train and bank holdups. But it wasn't until he was released from Rawlings Penitentiary, Wyoming, that he decided to get his own gang together. They soon became known as the Wild Bunch.

Legend has it that Butch, eulogised by contemporary posters as a cheery, affable character, never shot directly at a man. When pursued by a posse he would always fire at the horses.

Trains were the specialty of Butch and his Wild Bunch. One day they scooped $30,000 from a Union Pacific express by detaching the last car and blowing it and the safe inside to smithereens. They followed this success with three more train raids until Pinkerton agents got on the gang's trail.

Harry Sundance

The Pinkertons and the railroad's own crime fighters forced the gang to seek refuge in South America. Around 1909 (some say in Bolivia, others in Uruguay), Butch and his chief cohort in crime, Harry 'Sundance' Longbaugh, either committed suicide or were shot dead in a battle with troops.

Harry Longbaugh had got his nickname when, as a boy, he served eighteen months in jail at Sundance, Cook County, Wyoming, for horse stealing. Thereafter, he called himself the Sundance Kid.

The Kid had no raindrops falling on his head – only 'wanted' posters. In late 1901, Sundance and his lady love, Etta Place, sailed for Buenos Aires after being run out of the US by the Pinkertons.

He continued robbing banks and trains, managing to keep one step ahead of the law by hiding out among local Indians, until his death alongside Butch Cassidy.

Billy the Kid

The most famous gunfighter of the West was a soft-spoken, agreeable young man named William Bonney, better known as Billy the Kid. Believed to have been born in New York, he moved west with his family and became a cowboy in Lincoln County, New Mexico. There he worked for an English ranch owner John Tunstall, who befriended him.

In March 1878, two killers riding with the posse of corrupt Sheriff Brady of Pecos blasted Tunstall to death. When Bonney, then aged nineteen, heard of his benefactor's death, he grabbed a pair of Colt 44s and went looking for the two killers.

Billy found them and shot them dead. Then, with a price on his head, he teamed up with a gang whose members put paid to Sheriff Brady.

By now, Bonney's fame was spreading. People began talking about a gunslinger named Billy the Kid.

State Governor Wallace tried to con Billy into giving himself up. Wallace hired the Kid's one-time friend, Pat Garrett, who persuaded Billy to testify at an inquiry into gang warfare in Lincoln County in exchange for a light sentence.

The Kid walked smack into the trap – but shot his way to freedom. Unknown to Billy, Garrett was made Sheriff of Lincoln County in recognition of his treachery.

Still trading on their old friendship, Garrett guessed that eventually the Kid would head towards the hideout of a mutual friend, Pete Maxwell.

Garrett got there first, urging Maxwell to persuade Billy to surrender. But as they were talking, Billy walked in – straight into two slugs from Garrett's Colt.

Billy the Kid, twenty-one, sprawled dead with nineteen notches on his gun. But he could never add up. He had actually killed twenty-one people in less than two years to avenge his friend and earn himself a place in American legend.

Black Bart

The Wild West is packed with stories of vicious outlaws. But one robber who stood apart was Black Bart. He was always courteous, never hurt anybody and stole only from the treasure box and mailbags, never from the passengers.

Bart's first holdup was on a blazing hot day in 1875 when he stopped a Wells Fargo stagecoach near Sonora, California. As the horses struggled up a hill, a strange armed man jumped out from the bushes. He wore a flour sack on his head, with holes cut out for the eyes, and a long, white coat.

He ordered the driver to throw down the box and mailbags, and shouted to his hidden accomplices to shoot if anyone offered resistance. The driver saw six guns poking out from the bushes. They were all trained on the stagecoach.

What followed that day has passed into Western folklore. For when a petrified woman passenger threw her purse at Bart's feet, he calmly picked it up. With a gracious bow, he returned the purse and said he was interested only in the treasure box and mailbags. Not passengers' money or valuables. The strange robber took his loot and told the driver to continue his journey.

For several years, Black Bart robbed in his cavalier manner. His reputation and courteous ways became the talk of California. And he never earned more than £250 from each of his stagecoach robberies, since most gold and valuables were by then transported by train.

The man given the task of nailing Black Bart was Jim Hume, Wells Fargo's chief detective.

He soon realised that Bart was cunning and resourceful. When he visited the scene of that first robbery, Bart's 'gang' were still there – six sticks poking through the bushes.

Hume learned little about Bart. He left no clues, his trail just petered out and he seemed to walk everywhere rather than ride.

Bart became bolder and even left Hume his name and a poem at the scene of one of his crimes. Then Black Bart began to slip up.

After a series of holdups, Hume visited houses in the area and learned that a grey-haired, hitchhiking stranger with a grey beard, white moustache and two missing front teeth had stopped to have dinner. A picture of the hooded raider was at last emerging.

A laundry mark on a handkerchief finally led to Black Bart's capture in 1882. The thief managed to escape unharmed when he was interrupted by a young gunman as he was about to rob a coach. But he blundered by leaving his sleeping roll and his handkerchief.

Jim Hume had no trouble tracing the laundry mark to a San Francisco laundry – and that led him to a Mr. Bolton. He was an elderly man, softly spoken, with grey hair, grey beard, white moustache and two missing front teeth.

Mr. Bolton explained his long absences from home by saying that he had to make frequent visits to his mine. But there was no mine, and Jim Hume knew he had his man when Black Bart's clothes were found at Bolton's home.

Black Bart was arrested and, courteous to the end, returned much of the money taken on his raids. For their part, Wells Fargo made charges only on one holdup and forgot about the others.

By now, the gentlemanly thief had become a popular hero. The judge must have had a soft spot for him, too. He was jailed for six years. It could have been worse.

Black Bart Bolton may have been one of the last stagecoach robbers – but he is remembered first and foremost as the outlaw who wouldn't hurt a fly.

✿✿

Confidence Trickster – Frank Abagnale

Frank William Abagnale, Jr. (born April 27, 1948) is an American security consultant best known for his history as a former confidence trickster, cheque forger, skilled impostor, and escape artist. He became notorious in the 1960s for successfully passing US $4.5 million worth of meticulously forged cheques across twenty-six countries over the course of five years, beginning when he was sixteen-years-old.

In the process, he claimed to have assumed no fewer than eight separate identities, successfully impersonating an airline pilot, a doctor, a Bureau of Prisons agent and a lawyer. He escaped from police custody twice (once from a taxiing airliner and once from a US federal penitentiary), all before he was twenty-one -years-old. Abagnale's life story provided the inspiration for the feature film *Catch Me If You Can*, and he elaborated on his life through his ghostwritten autobiography of the same name. He is currently a consultant and lecturer at the academy and field offices for the Federal Bureau of Investigation. He also runs Abagnale & Associates, a financial fraud consultancy company.

Childhood

Abagnale was born the third of five children and spent the first sixteen years of his life in Bronxville, New York. His French mother, Paulette, and father, Frank Abagnale Sr., divorced when he was sixteen, and afterwards he would be the only child of whom his father would gain custody. At the divorce hearing, Abagnale ran away never to see his father again. According to Abagnale, his father did not necessarily want him, but to reunite his family, he would attempt to win his mother back until his father's death in 1974. His father was also an affluent local who was very keen on politics, and was a major role model for Abagnale Jr.

First con

His first victim was his father. As Frank Jr. grew interested in women, he found that he could not stop spending money on them. To fund his exploits with the opposite sex, since he was always short on cash, he asked his father for a credit card on which to charge gas for the 1962 Ford truck his father gave him. He began to make deals with gas station employees all around the New York area to falsely charge items to his card, then give him a portion of the money; in return the employee got to keep the item and "resell" it for the full price. Over the course of two months, Frank Jr. "bought" 14 sets of tires, 22 batteries, and large quantities of gasoline.

The bill totalled US $3,400, which his father discovered only after a debt collector contacted him in person, as Frank Jr. was throwing away the bills that came in the mail. According to *Catch Me If You Can*, Frank Sr. was not angered with his son over the charges rung up, but merely puzzled as to his motive. Both he and the bill collector sympathised when Frank Jr. explained that "It's the girls, Dad, they do funny things to me. I can't explain it." However, Frank Jr. decided to rethink his ways and find new quick cash ideas, mainly because he saw that the gas card scam had hurt Frank Sr., a man he viewed as a hardworking businessman.

Bank Fraud

Abagnale's first confidence trick was writing personal cheque on his own overdrawn account. This, however, would only work for a limited time before the bank demanded payment, so he moved on to opening other accounts in different banks, eventually creating new identities to sustain this charade.

Over time, he experimented and developed different ways of defrauding banks, such as printing out his own almost-perfect copies of cheques, depositing them and persuading banks to advance him cash on the basis of money in his accounts.

One of Abagnale's famous tricks was to print his account number on blank deposit slips and add them to the stack of real blank slips in the bank. This meant that the deposits written on those slips by bank customers ended up going into his account rather than that of the legitimate customers.

At a speech given to the students of Florida State University, Frank described one instance where he noticed the location where airlines and car rental businesses such as United Airlines and Hertz would drop off their daily collections of money in a zip-up bag and deposit it into a drop box on the airport premises. Using a security guard disguise he bought at a local costume shop, he put a sign over the box saying "out of service, place deposits with security guard on duty" and collected money that way. Later he disclosed how he could not believe this idea had actually worked, stating with some astonishment: "how can a drop box be out of service?"

Impersonations

Airline Pilot

Pan American World Airways estimated that between the ages of 16 and 18, Frank Abagnale flew over 1,000,000 miles on over 250 flights and flew to 26 countries, at Pan Am's expense, by deadheading. He was also able to stay at hotels for free during this time. Everything from food to lodging was billed to the airline. Abagnale stated that although he was often invited by actual pilots to take the controls in flight, he never actually accepted their offers, instead using the "8 hours between the bottle and the throttle" rule as a convenient alibi.

Teaching Assistant

He forged a Columbia University degree and taught sociology at Brigham Young University for a semester, working as a teaching assistant by the name of "Frank Adams".

Doctor

For nearly a year, he impersonated a chief resident pediatrician in a Georgia hospital under the alias of Frank Conners. He chose to do this after nearly being caught by police after leaving a flight in New Orleans. Aware of possible capture, he retired to Georgia for the time being. When filling out an application for an apartment he listed his previous occupation as "doctor" fearing that the owner might check with Pan Am if he had listed "pilot". After becoming friends with a real doctor who lived beneath him, he became a resident supervisor of interns as a favour for him until they found someone who could take the job. He did not find the job difficult because supervisors did not have to do any actual medical work. However, as a medical layman, Abagnale was nearly discovered after almost letting a baby die through oxygen deprivation (he had no idea what the nurse meant when she said there was a "blue baby"). Abagnale was able to fake his way through most of his duties by letting the interns handle most of the cases that came in during his late night shift, for example setting broken bones and other such tasks. Finally, the hospital found another replacement and he returned to the air. In an interview, he said that the supervisor had a death in the family and had to fly out West, during which Abagnale took the position. However, since they had trouble finding a permanent applicant, he stayed for three years.

Attorney

Abagnale forged a Harvard University law transcript, passed the bar exam of Louisiana and got a job at the office of the state attorney general of Louisiana at the age of nineteen. This happened while he was posing as Pan Am First Officer "Robert Black". He told a stewardess he had briefly dated that he was also a Harvard law student and she introduced him to a lawyer friend. Abagnale was told the bar needed more lawyers and was offered a chance to apply. After making a fake transcript from Harvard, he prepared himself for the compulsory exam. Despite failing twice, he claims to have passed the bar exam legitimately on the third try after 8 weeks of study, because "Louisiana at the time allowed you to take the Bar over and over as many times as you needed. It was really a matter of eliminating what you got wrong."

In his biography, he described the premise of his legal job as a "gopher boy" who simply fetched coffee and books for his boss. However, there was a real Harvard graduate who also worked for that attorney general, and he hounded Abagnale with questions about his tenure at Harvard. Naturally, Abagnale could not answer questions about a university he had never attended, and he later resigned after eight months to protect himself, after learning the suspicious graduate was making inquiries into his background.

Capture and Imprisonment

Eventually, he was caught in France in 1969 when an Air France attendant whom he had dated in the past recognised him and notified the police. When the French police apprehended him, twelve of the countries in which he had committed fraud sought his extradition. After a two-day trial, he first served prison time in Perpignan's House of Arrest in France—a one-year sentence that was reduced by the presiding judge at his trial to six months. His stay in Perpignan left him fearful of spending more time in another version of the prison.

He was then extradited to Sweden where he was treated fairly well under Swedish law. During trial for forgery, his defense attorney almost had his case dismissed by arguing that he had "created" the fake cheques and not forged them, but his charges were instead reduced to swindling and fraud. He served six months in a Malmö prison, only to learn at the end of it he would be tried next in Italy. Later, a Swedish judge asked a U.S. State Department official to revoke his passport. Without a valid passport Swedish authorities were legally compelled to deport him to the U.S., where he was sentenced to twelve years in a federal prison for multiple counts of forgery.

Alleged Escapes

While being extradited to the U.S., Abagnale escaped from a British VC-10 airliner as it was turning onto a taxi strip at New York's JFK International Airport. Under cover of night, he scaled a nearby fence and hailed a cab to Grand Central Terminal. After stopping in the Bronx to change clothes and pick up a set of keys to a Montreal bank safe deposit box containing US $20,000, Abagnale caught a train to Montreal's Dorval Airport (now Montreal-Pierre Elliot Trudeau International Airport) to purchase a ticket to São Paulo, Brazil, a country with which the U.S. had no extradition treaty. On his way to Montreal he had a close call at a Mac's Milk in Dundas, Ontario. He was caught by a constable of the Royal Canadian Mounted Police while standing in line at the ticket counter and subsequently handed over to the U.S. Border Patrol.

Being sentenced to twelve years in the Federal Correction Institution at Petersburg, Virginia, in April 1971, Abagnale also reportedly escaped the Federal Detention Center in Atlanta, Georgia while awaiting trial, which he considers in his book to be one of the most infamous escapes in history. During the time, U.S. prisons were being condemned by civil rights groups and investigated by congressional committees. In a stroke of luck that included the accompanying U.S. marshal forgetting his detention commitment papers, Abagnale was mistaken for an undercover prison inspector and was even given privileges and food far better than the other inmates. The FDC in Atlanta had already lost two employees as a result of reports written by undercover federal agents, and Abagnale took advantage of their vulnerability. He contacted a friend (called in his book "Jean Sebring") who posed as his fiancée and slipped him the business card of "Inspector C.W. Dunlap" of the Bureau of Prisons which she had obtained by posing as a freelance writer doing an article on "fire safety measures in federal detention centers". She also handed over a business card from "Sean O'Riley" (later revealed to be Joe Shea), the FBI agent in charge of Abagnale's case, which she doctored at a stationery print shop. Abagnale told the corrections officers that he was indeed a prison inspector and handed over Dunlap's business card as proof. He told them that he needed to contact FBI Agent Sean O'Riley, on a matter of urgent business.

O'Riley's phone number (actually the number altered by Sebring) was dialled and picked up by Jean Sebring, at a payphone in an Atlanta shopping mall, posing as an operator at the Federal Bureau of Investigation. Later, he was allowed to meet unsupervised with O'Riley in a predetermined car outside the detention center. Sebring, incognito, picked Abagnale up and drove him to an Atlanta bus station where he took a Greyhound bus to New York, and soon thereafter, a train to Washington, D.C. Abagnale bluffed his way through an attempted capture by posing as an FBI agent after being recognised by a motel registration clerk. Still bent on making his way to Brazil, Abagnale was picked up a few weeks later by two New York City Police Department detectives when he inadvertently walked past their unmarked police car.

Legitimate Jobs

In 1974, after he had served less than five years, the United States federal government released him on the condition that he would help the federal authorities without pay against crimes committed by fraud and scam artists, and sign in once a week. Not wanting to return to his family in New York, he left the choice of parole up to the court, and it was decided that he would be paroled in Texas.

After his release, Abagnale tried several jobs, including cook, grocer and movie projectionist, but he was fired from most of these upon having his criminal career discovered via background checks and not informing his employers that he was a former convict. Finding them unsatisfying, he approached a bank with an offer. He explained to the bank what he had done, and offered to speak to the bank's staff and show various tricks that "paperhangers" use to defraud banks. His offer included the condition that if they did not find his speech helpful, they would owe him nothing; otherwise, they would only owe him $50, with an agreement that they would provide his name to other banks. The banks were impressed by the results, and he began a legitimate life as a security consultant.

He later founded Abagnale & Associates, which advises businesses on fraud. Abagnale is now a millionaire through his legal fraud detection and avoidance consulting business based in Tulsa, Oklahoma. Abagnale also continues to advise the FBI, with whom he has associated for over thirty-five years, by teaching at the FBI Academy and lecturing for FBI field offices throughout the country. According to his website, more than

14,000 institutions have adopted Abagnale's fraud prevention programs.

He lives in Tulsa, Oklahoma with his wife, whom he married one year after becoming legitimate. They have three sons, including one who currently works for the FBI.

Joe Shea, the FBI agent on whom the character of Carl Hanratty was based for the film *Catch Me If You Can*, remains a close friend.

Veracity of Claims

The authenticity of Abagnale's criminal exploits were questioned even before the publishing of *Catch Me If You Can*. In 1978, after Abagnale had been a featured speaker at an anti-crime seminar, a *San Francisco Chronicle* reporter looked into his assertions. Phone calls to banks, schools, hospitals and other institutions Abagnale mentioned turned up no evidence of his cons under the aliases he used. Abagnale's response was that "Due to the embarrassment involved, I doubt if anyone would confirm the information."

In 2002, Abagnale himself addressed the issue of his story's truthfulness rather vaguely with a statement posted on his company's website. The statement said in part "I was interviewed by the co-writer only about four times. I believe he did a great job of telling the story, but he also over dramatised and exaggerated some of the story. That was his style and what the editor wanted. He always reminded me that he was just telling a story and not writing my biography."

Media Appearances

In 1977, Abagnale appeared on the TV quiz show *To Tell the Truth*, along with two contestants also presenting themselves as him. A reenactment of this episode appeared in *Catch Me if You Can*, featuring actor Leonardo DiCaprio in his place.

In the early 1990s, Abagnale was featured as a recurring guest on the UK Channel 4 television series *Secret Cabaret*. The show was based around magic and illusions with a sinister, almost gothic presentation style. Abagnale was featured as an expert exposing various confidence tricks.

Leonardo DiCaprio portrayed Abagnale in the 2002 Steven Spielberg film *Catch Me if You Can*. The film is based on his exploits as described in his book of the same name, but alters many aspects of his life story for dramatic purposes. The real Abagnale makes a cameo appearance in this film as one of the French police officers taking his character into custody.

In 2007, Abagnale appeared in a short role as a speaker in the BBC TV series *The Real Hustle*. He spoke of different scams run by fraudsters.

Mysterious Anastasia

Tsar Nicholas II rose uneasily to his feet as the door burst open and the cellar filled with grim-faced men carrying revolvers and bayonets. At their head stood Jacob Yurovsky, the Russian Royal family's gaoler. He quickly read out a few words from a piece of paper clutched in his hand: it was an execution order, signed by the Ekaterinburg Soviet.

The Tsar started to protest, but Yurovsky was already giving the order to fire. Nicholas died first, vainly trying to shield his wife, Alexandra. Those not killed by the bullets were stabbed, pathetically attempting to ward off the thrusts with cushions. It was soon over. None had been spared. Even the family's pet spaniel had been clubbed to death. The Tsar, his immediate family, their physician and two servants lay in a tangled, bloody heap on the floor.

The bodies were left in the cellar for a few days, and then they were taken out, soaked in gasoline, burnt beyond recognition and thrown down a disused mine shaft. The grisly remains were discovered eleven days later by soldiers of the White Armies, when they captured Ekaterinburg on July 27, 1918. There was, of course, an international outcry against this latest Soviet atrocity. Lenin's Moscow government denied responsibility and ignored the protests. But their blame was never in doubt, as the subsequent murders of other members of the Imperial Romanov family proved.

Improbable Story

Those supporters of the Tsar who remained alive fled and established aristocratic but poverty-stricken little groups throughout the capitals of Europe. And it was to one such group in Berlin that a woman, telling a strange and improbable story, presented herself in 1920. Giving her name as Madame Tchaikovsky, she claimed that she was in fact the Grand

Duchess Anastasia, youngest daughter of the Tsar. Not everyone, it seemed, had died in the cellar. . . .

The Berlin Tsarists were led by Prince Constantine Gabriel, and he was impressed with "Anastasia". So too was Gleb Botkin, whose father was the physician who had been killed with the Royal family. Madame Tchaikovsky's story was certainly gripping. She said that she had miraculously escaped both the bullets and the bayonets and had been rescued from the cellar by a soldier called Tchaikovsky. They had then made off together in a covered wagon while the Bolsheviks searched frantically for the missing body.

After crossing war-torn Russia, they arrived in Bucharest, where "Madame Tchaikovsky" gave birth to a child. It was the shame of this, she said, which prevented her from contacting her Rumanian relatives. Tchaikovsky then disappeared. No one knows where, although it was later rumoured that he had been murdered by Soviet agents. Madame Tchaikovsky decided the only thing she could do was make her way to Berlin and seek safety and recognition there.

Incredible though her story was, there were a great many influential people, such as Gabriel and Botkin, prepared to believe it; there were others, notably her paternal aunt, the Grand Duchess Olga and the Grand Duke Andrew, who believed her at first but changed their minds later.

Those who championed Madame Tchaikovsky alleged that her detractors were motivated solely by greed. It was thought, although never verified, that the Tsar had deposited millions of roubles with the Bank of England; if Madame Tchaikovsky could indisputably prove her identity as the Tsar's closest surviving relative, then this fortune would presumably pass to her and not the Romanovs.

Mentally Unbalanced

No matter how many times she was questioned, Madame Tchaikovsky's story never changed, and soon she was being accorded the honours due a Tsar's daughter. This did not, however, stop her attempting to kill herself a short time later, and rumours began to the effect that she had become mentally unbalanced. In a curious way, though, this strengthened people's belief in her, and their belief was endorsed by other events. A former nurse to the Royal family was introduced to Madame Tchaikovsky and immediately vowed that she was the real Anastasia. Gleb Botkin persistently supported her claim. After all, he said, did we not play together as children?

But the Grand Dukes Cyril—who proclaimed himself "Protector of the Russian Throne" in 1922—and Boris remained determinedly unconvinced, and Captain Djamgaroff, another refugee, was also scornful of Madame Tchaikovsky. He said: "It has not been definitely proved who she really is. But there can be no doubt that she is insane, suffering from a persecution mania with its customary symptom—the delusion of grandeur."

A few years later a woman called Frau von Ratieff published her memoirs. The book not only stated that Madame Tchaikovsky was Anastasia but also accused the Grand Dukes Cyril and Boris of actively plotting her discredit. If Madame Tchaikovsky was really who she said she was, they would no longer be able to feel secure as the heads of the surviving Imperial family; certain material benefits fell their way because of their position, and, said Fran Ratieff, they were understandably loath to give them up.

During this period there were several other claimants to the name "Grand Duchess Anastasia", and the situation became more and more confused. Then someone had the idea of subjecting the case to scientific scrutiny. By that time the French system of Bertillonage, relying as it did on anthropometric measurements, was widely accepted as an almost infallible method of establishing a person's identity. Why not put Madame Tchaikovsky to the test?

Possibly the leading exponent of Bertillonage was Professor Mark Bischoff, Director of the Institute of Scientific Police at Lausanne in Switzerland; and in January 1927 he was asked if he would solve the mystery. He was supplied with a number of photographs of the Grand Duchess Anastasia herself and Madame Tchaikovsky.

Absolutely Determined

The work was to take him eight months and involved him in not only detailed studies of Madame Tchaikovsky and Anastasia but also in comparisons between them and other members of the Russian Royal family. He was absolutely determined to prove the question of identity one way or the other. Professor Bischoff was especially interested in the length of the subjects' ears and the distance between the chin and middle of the eyebrows.

A profile of Anastasia and one of Madame Tchaikovsky were scaled down and partially superimposed, rather like the heads on a stamp or coin. Professor Bischoff first placed Anastasia's profile uppermost with Madame Tchaikovsky's behind and then reversed them. By doing this he was able to detect noticeable differences in the two outlines.

However, he was not yet satisfied, and so turned his attentions on the two ladies' ears. He studied photographs of Anastasia taken at different times, including one just before the Ekaterinburg murders. In all of them the ears were identical. He reduced it to two. In both photographs the right ear was shown to be narrow at the outside edge and only slightly convoluted in the wide top half area. But Madame Tchaikovsky's right ear was much broader at the edge and more convoluted.

This was the breakthrough Professor Bischoff had been waiting for. The test seemed absolutely conclusive. He was convinced that the woman calling herself Madame Tchaikovsky was not Anastasia; she was an impostor, and he had no hesitation in denouncing her as one. Madame Tchaikovsky was finished. Suddenly, she found no one wanted to know her, and her erstwhile supporters melted mysteriously away. There seemed nothing she could do except leave Europe.

She was invited to visit the United States as the guest of a former Russian princess and set sail—travelling incognito —on the liner *Berengaria*. She refused to have anything to do with the other passengers and remained isolated in her cabin throughout the entire voyage. Naturally, her fellow voyagers were intrigued, and the rumours surrounding the mysterious and secretive lady preceded the ship to New York.

When Madame Tchaikovsky went on shore she was greeted by a large group of newspaper reporters and photographers, but she steadfastly refused to answer any of their questions. She had, however, been recognised. The next day all the newspapers carried headlines announcing the arrival of the "Grand Duchess".

Within a short time the controversy over her identity became again a matter for public debate, and the newspapers were filled with argument and counterargument. Several of them published a photograph of Madame Tchaikovsky which had been given to them after her arrival in America. A copy of this particular photograph was sent to Professor Bischoff in Switzerland. He applied the same exhaustive tests, but this time the results were different: the ears were the same.

No whit perturbed, he issued the following statement: "From this evidence the alleged portrait of Madame Tchaikovsky appearing in the New York *Evening Post* of February 7, 1928, is a retouched reproduction of the photograph of the Grand Duchess Anastasia Nikolaievna!" This appeared to be the end for Madame Tchaikovsky and her persistent claims. She returned to Germany, changed her name to Anna Anderson and spent the rest of her life as a recluse.

After the Second World War there was a revival of interest in the Anastasia story. A play was produced in the 1950s and the authors even gave Anna Anderson a share of the royalties; 20th Century-Fox made a film, and countless magazines ran feature articles.

Amazingly Detailed

In 1963, a woman in Chicago announced that she was the Grand Duchess Anastasia. She was called Eugenia Smith, and she did, in fact, have an amazingly detailed knowledge of the Imperial court. She said she had been rescued from the cellar by an officer, later married a Croatian and made her way to New York in 1922, where she became a model. Her story was convincing enough but later discounted. Using the Bertillonage method, a Harvard anthropologist proved she was a fraud.

The last indisputably genuine Russian Grand Duchesses—Xenia, living in London, and Olga in Canada—died within a few months of each other in 1960.

It was astonishingly claimed in 1964 by a C.I.A. agent that he was Tsar Nicholas's only son Alexis, and that the whole murder story was a piece of complex Communist subterfuge. He said that the Royal family had escaped to Poland. The Tsar had died in 1924, the Tsarina in 1952, and that all the daughters were still alive.

The Great Imposter Ferdinand Waldo Demara

Ferdinand Waldo Demara, Jr., known as "the Great Impostor", masqueraded as many people from monks to surgeons to prison wardens. He was the subject of a movie, *The Great Impostor*, in which he was played by Tony Curtis.

During Demara's "careers," he was, among other things, a ship's doctor, a civil engineer, a sheriff's deputy, an assistant prison warden, a doctor of applied psychology, a hospital orderly, a lawyer, a childcare expert, a Benedictine monk, a Trappist monk, an editor, a cancer researcher, and a teacher. One teaching job led to six months in prison. He never seemed to get (or seek) much monetary gain in what he was doing – just temporary respectability.

Many of Demara's unsuspecting employers, under other circumstances, would have been satisfied with Demara as an employee. Demara was said to possess a true photographic memory and was widely reputed to have an extraordinary IQ. He was apparently able to memorise necessary techniques from textbooks and worked on two cardinal rules: *The burden of proof is on the accuser* and *When in danger, attack*. He described his own motivation as "Rascality, pure rascality".

Early Life and Adulthood

Demara, known locally as "Fred", was born in Lawrence, Massachusetts in 1921, at 40 Texas Avenue in the lower southwest Tower Hill Neighbourhood. His father, Ferdinand Waldo Demara, Sr. was born in Rhode Island and worked in Lawrence's old Theatre District as a motion picture operator. Although his uncle, Napoleon Louis Demara, Sr. owned those theatres, Fred's father, Ferdinand, Sr. was an active union member.

Fred ran away from home at the age of sixteen to join Cistercian monks in Rhode Island, where he stayed for several years. He joined the U.S. Army in 1941.

Impersonations

The following year Demara began his new lives by borrowing the name of Anthony Ignolia, an army buddy, and went AWOL. After two more tries in monasteries, he joined the Navy. He did not reach the position he wanted, faked his suicide and borrowed another name, Robert Linton French, and became a religiously-oriented psychologist. He taught psychology in a Pennsylvania college, served as an orderly in a Los Angeles sanitarium, as an instructor in St. Martin's College in the state of Washington. The FBI caught him eventually and he served eighteen months in prison for desertion.

After his release, he assumed a fake identity and studied law at night at Northeastern University, then joined the Brothers of Christian Instruction in Maine, a Roman Catholic order.

While at the Brothers of Christian Instruction, he became acquainted with a young doctor named Joseph C. Cyr. That led to his most famous exploit, in which he masqueraded as Dr. Cyr, working as a trauma surgeon aboard the HMCS Cayuga, a Royal Canadian Navy destroyer, during the Korean War. He managed to improvise successful major surgeries and fend off infection with generous amounts of penicillin. His most notable surgical practices were performed on some sixteen Korean combat casualties who were loaded onto the Cayuga. All eyes turned to Demara, the only "surgeon" on board, as it became obvious that several of the casualties would require major surgery or certainly die. After ordering personnel to transport these variously injured patients into the ship's operating room and prep them for surgery, Demara disappeared to his room with a textbook on general surgery and proceeded to speed-read the various surgeries he was now forced to perform, including major chest surgery. None of the casualties died as a result of Demara's surgeries. Apparently, the removal of a bullet from a wounded man ended up in Canadian newspapers. One person reading the reports was the mother of the real Dr. Joseph Cyr; her son at the time of "his" service in Korea was actually practicing medicine in Grand Falls, New Brunswick. When news of the impostor reached the *Cayuga,* still on duty off Korea, Captain James Plomer at first refused to believe Demara was not a doctor (and not Joseph Cyr). The Canadian Navy chose not to press charges, and Demara returned to the United States.

Minor fame

After this episode, he sold his tale to *Life* magazine and worked in short-term jobs, since he was now widely known. He resorted to drinking. Only after he returned to his old tricks and got fake credentials could he get another job at a prison in Huntsville, Texas. According to his biographer, Demara's past became known and his position untenable when an inmate found a copy of *Life* with an article about the impostor.

He continued to use new aliases but as a result of his self-generated publicity, impersonation was harder to accomplish than before. In 1960, as a publicity stunt, Demara was given a small acting role in the horror film *The Hypnotic Eye.* He appears briefly in the film as a (genuine) hospital surgeon. Ironically, the impostor who fooled so many people in real life reveals a total lack of acting ability in this brief role. By this point, Demara's girth was so notable that he could not avoid attracting attention. Demara had already been considerably overweight during his impersonation of Cyr.

Later life

In the early 60s, Demara worked as a counselor at the Union Rescue Mission in downtown Los Angeles. In 1967, Demara received a Graduate Certificate in Bible from Multnomah Bible College in Portland, Oregon.

Demara had various friendships with a wide variety of notable people during his life. This included a close relationship with actor Steve McQueen, to whom Demara delivered last rites in November 1980.

When Demara's past exploits and infamy were discovered in the late 1970s, he was almost dismissed from the Good Samaritan Hospital in Anaheim, California where he worked as a visiting chaplain. Chief of Staff Dr. Philip S. Cifarelli, who had developed a close personal friendship with Demara, personally vouched for him and Demara was allowed to remain as Chaplain. Demara was a very active and appreciated minister, serving a variety of patients in the hospital. Few of those with whom he interacted at the hospital knew of his colourful past. Due to limited financial resources and his friendships with Cifarelli and Dr. Jerry Nielson, Demara was allowed to live in the hospital until his death, even after illness forced him to stop working for them in 1980.

Demara died on June 7, 1982 due to heart failure and complications from his diabetic condition which required both of his legs to be amputated. According to his obituary in the New York Times, he had been living in Orange County, California, for eight years.

In media

Demara's story was recounted in the 1960 book, *The Great Impostor,* written by Robert Crichton and published by Random House; the book was a New York Times bestseller and adapted into a 1961 film by the same name starring Tony Curtis as Demara. A second book by Crichton, *The Rascal and the Road*, recounted Demara and Crichton's experiences together as Crichton conducted research for "The Great Impostor."

The Clerk who 'Invested' his Bank's £32 Million

Marc Colombo was a little man with big ideas. As a lowly foreign exchange dealer working for a British bank in Switzerland, he saw fortunes changing hands daily. Fluctuations in the values of the world's leading currencies opened up enticing opportunities for men shrewd and brave enough to buy when the price was right and sell at a profit.

Colombo, a handsome twenty-eight-year-old, was one of only 16 employees at the Lugano branch of Lloyds Bank International. Lugano was the smallest of the organisation's 170 branches—yet after Marco Colombo had finished with it, its name was better known than any other in the world!

The Middle East war of 1973 led to an oil embargo by Arab states. This sent foreign exchange rates crazy and made Colombo believe that the dollar's value would tumble while the Swiss franc remained strong. So he struck what is known as a forward deal with other international money dealers.

In November 1973, he agreed that—at current rates his bank would buy US $34 million with Swiss francs the following January. He thought that the dollar's value would have fallen by that time and he would be able to use cheap dollars to buy back his francs. But instead the dollar went from strength to strength.

He now realised he had cost Lloyds about £I million. He wasn' t too worried. After all, his bank had just declared half-yearly profits £78 million.

One person who had to be kept in the dark, however, was the bank manager, Egidio Mombelli. Having worked for Mombelli for a year, Colombo knew that, if he kept up a show of confidence, his boss would not suspect a thing. But he had to recoup his losses.

Without Lloyd's knowledge, Colombo continued to speculate. After pinning his faith on the dollar falling, which it did not, he changed his tactics, believing it would go on rising. Instead it eventually fell.

Lloyds had a £700,000 daily limit on debts or holdings. Colombo went way above this. The only records he kept were in his diary. The bank and the Swiss banking authorities had no clue as to what was going on. And neither did his colleagues or the unfortunate Mombelli. To them, Colombo was a hardworking, trustworthy employee.

But everything changed in August, 1974. It was then that a Lloyds Bank man in London was told by a top French banker that their Lugano branch had 'reached its limit with us'. Lloyds' offices in Queen Victoria Street were on the alert. Phone calls showed that a German bank had also been doing huge currency deals with Lugano.

A plane from London took Lloyds chiefs to Lugano the next day. They interviewed Colombo, Mombelli and the man in charge of all three of Lloyds' Swiss branches, Karl Senft. A mass of documents and the three Swiss employees accompanied the bankers back to London.

It took a full weekend to sort out the mess. At the end, Lloyds men were shocked to find that there was £235 million still tied up in the dangerous 'forward' deals. Colombo had believed in putting all his golden eggs in one basket. A sum greater than the combined capital and reserves of all three Lloyds banks in Switzerland was staked. The bank records had shown a mere £36,000.

Lloyds had to call in the Bank of England to unscramble things. The Governor himself agreed to allow them to transfer vast quantities of money to Lugano so that the deals set up by Colombo would be honoured.

The bank's international money market director, Robert Gras, also had his work cut out. He had to buy in the dollars Colombo had agreed to sell, without people realising. It was a tricky operation which could be made vastly more expensive if international money men knew Lloyds were over a barrel.

It took three weeks of quietly feverish activity to settle the debts and, at the end, the world was told that Lloyds in Switzerland had lost a horrific £32 million. Never before – in Switzerland or in Britain – had such a loss been known. Lloyds' London shares immediately lost £20 million when chairman Sir Eric Faulkner broke the news.

By that time, Colombo and Mombelli and their families had gone into hiding away from the eager questioning of the Press.

A year later both appeared in Lugano's court on charges of criminal mismanagement, falsification of documents and violations of the Swiss banking code. Colombo denied that he had accepted illegal commissions or had any criminal intent, but he did admit breaking the dealing limits and conducting unauthorised transactions. He also slammed Lloyds Lugano branch for its lax systems of checking and criticised the 'frustrating' spending limits that had been placed on him. Colombo seemed unmoved when the prosecution described him as the 'mouse that made Lloyds tremble' and accused him of throwing money about like a man at a casino.

'Being a foreign exchange dealer is always a hazardous operation,' he told them. 'It is a gambler's profession.'

He was unrepentant about the extent of his speculation. 'There was the pride of the foreign exchange dealer who will not admit failure,' he told the court. 'I was at all times convinced that I could recoup my losses, but it only takes something a little unforeseen to upset the market. I was a prisoner of events.'

Even if Colombo had ended up with a profit he would still have faced the sack for breaking banking rules. But he claimed he would have netted £11 million for Lloyds if they had allowed his currency deals to stand.

Mombelli, 41, admitted that he had never understood what was happening and said he had signed papers without realising what they were.

'It's a foreign exchange Mafia,' Mombelli said after the trial. 'For every dealer you need at least four administrators to check what he is doing. They do things no ordinary banker understands.'

The two men walked from the court, much to Lloyds' amazement. Colombo received an eighteen month suspended sentence and Mombelli one of six months, with a £300 fine each. The judge accepted that the two had not been out to line their own pockets.

Six Degrees of Separation

David Hampton (April 4, 1964 – July 18, 2003) was an American con artist who gained infamy in the 1980s after milking a group of wealthy Manhattanites out of thousands of dollars by convincing them that he was Sidney Poitier's son. His story became the inspiration for a play and later a movie, titled *Six Degrees of Separation*.

Background

Hampton, eldest son of an attorney in Buffalo, moved to New York City in 1981 and stumbled upon his now-famous ruse in 1983, when he and a friend were trying to get into Studio 54. Unable to gain entry, Hampton's friend decided to pose as Gregory Peck's son, while Hampton assumed the identity of Sidney Poitier's son. They were ushered in as celebrities. Hampton began employing the persona of "David Poitier" to cadge free meals in restaurants. He also persuaded at least a dozen people into letting him stay with them in their homes or to give him money, including Melanie Griffith; Gary Sinise; Calvin Klein; John Jay Iselin, the president of WNET; Osborn Elliott, the dean of the Columbia University Graduate School of Journalism; and a Manhattan urologist. He told some of them that he was a friend of their children, some that he had just missed his plane to Los Angeles and that all his luggage was on it, some that his belongings had been stolen.

In October 1983, Hampton was arrested and convicted for his frauds and was ordered to pay restitution of $4,490 to his various victims. He was also banned from New York City. After he refused to comply with these terms, he was sentenced to a term of 18 months to 4 years in prison.

Due to eventual wider knowledge of the film *Six Degrees of Separation*, Hampton evolved other false identities and travelled

extensively to find new victims for his cons. Hampton was in and out of prison in numerous states, and was interviewed during each break from incarceration by a journalist with *The Justice Files*, seen in the USA on the Discovery Channel.

After swearing he had changed his life, Hampton continued travelling at least as late as 1996, where he found a large number of men who, even if they'd heard of his notoriety from the East Coast, had never seen his picture or the press, allowing him to move about unnoticed and work on numerous victims at one time. Example: in Spring 1996, Hampton arrived in Seattle, Washington, USA posing as Antonio de Montilio, the son of a wealthy District of Columbia physician. Due to his light skin colour, victims claimed he could easily be believed as the Puerto Rican he claimed. Typically, his story was colourful. Hampton claimed to have been mugged upon arriving in Seattle early for a work assignment for Vogue magazine. He was to interview Bill Gates but was suddenly in peril as his wallet was stolen and nothing could be replaced until that weekend was over. Hampton managed to woo two friends within blocks of each other without their being aware that he was working them both. It is believed that he was first drawn to one victim, Justin Baird, a local actor, since Baird had been identified at RPlace as the official taking in fundraising dollars from Bunny Brigade volunteers in that central location as they returned from their collection rounds.

Six Degrees of Separation

Playwright John Guare became interested in Hampton's story through his friendship with two of his duped hosts—Osborn and Inger Elliott, who were outraged to find "David Poitier" in bed with another man the morning after they let him into their home. *Six Degrees of Separation* opened at Lincoln Center in May 1990, and became a long-running success.

Hampton attempted to turn the play's success to his own advantage, giving interviews to the press, gate-crashing a producers' party, and beginning a campaign of harassment against Guare that included phone calls and death threats, prompting Guare to apply for a restraining order in April 1991, which was unsuccessful. In the fall of 1991, Hampton filed a $100 million lawsuit, claiming that the play had stolen the copyright on his persona and his story. His lawsuit was eventually dismissed.

Even after being caught as a con artist, Hampton continued his life of crime by duping a play coordinator. He claimed that he was the actor playing David Hampton in the successful play *Six Degrees of Separation*, but when caught, he denied knowing the play coordinator.

In 2003, David Hampton died of AIDS-related complications while being treated for his illness in a Manhattan hospital.

The 'Count' from the Backstreets of Sicily

For seven years, Count Cagliostro dazzled the high society of Europe's most fashionable cities. Royal courts marvelled as his magic elixirs performed apparent miracle cures. Scientists gasped at the gold and gems he could seemingly create from ordinary metal. Religious leaders believed him when he spoke of conversations with Moses and Solomon. London, Paris and Strasbourg were bewitched by his glittering lifestyle.

Tales of his achievements spread like wildfire. A Baltic state offered him its throne. Ministers at the Tsar's Moscow court lined up relatives for him to heal.

Then, in France, he was thrown into the Bastille for a crime of which he was innocent. And shocked princes and priests learned that the count they had feted was not what he seemed.

He was, in fact, a humble Sicilian named Giuseppe Balsamo. Born in a poverty-stricken backstreet of Palermo, in 1743, he had been living on his wits since stealing enough money from the church poor box and his uncle's savings to flee the island. He roamed the Mediterranean, staying for a while in Egypt, before settling to a lucrative life of crime in Rome, peddling homemade beauty creams and aphrodisiacs, copying paintings, forging banknotes and wills.

Here he met and married Lorenza Feliciani, a beautiful fifteen-year-old slum girl. Lorenza became the bait to lure rich victims into Balsamo's clutches. She was to help him reach the heights of fame and fortune, and send him tumbling to disgrace.

It was 1777 when the couple arrived in London. Rome had become too hot for them after a series of spectacular confidence tricks, and they had wandered for ten years through southern Europe and North Africa, perfecting the art of deception. Now they were ready for the big time.

Overnight, Giuseppe and Lorenza Balsamo became Count Alessandrio di Cagliostro and Countess Serafina. He claimed he had stolen her from an Oriental harem. They lived up to their titles with the richest clothes and jewellery, elegant coaches and hordes of servants in sumptuous livery. When people asked where their money came from, admirers whispered that the Count had the power to turn base metals into gold.

The truth was more prosaic. The couple had arrived with £3,000, the proceeds of their Mediterranean adventures.

But shortly after arriving in London, Balsamo had joined a London lodge of Freemasons. Such Orders were spreading quickly throughout the Continent, with the richest, noblest men clamouring to join. Balsamo progressed quickly, being elected Grand Master of his lodge. And that opened many doors to him in Europe when he began travelling.

In Paris, he invented what he called an 'Egyptian Rite' order of Freemasonry, appointing himself head as Grand Cophta. This entitled him to collect heavy initiation fees and membership dues. And whereas Freemasonry was for men only, he opened a female lodge, with Lorenza in charge as the new Queen of Sheba.

Gullible Parisians flocked to join, lured by the promise of learning some of the Grand Cophta's secrets. The Queen of Sheba confided to duchesses that though she looked thirty – which she was – she was really sixty. Her husband's magic five-drop potion kept her looking young.

Listeners promised to keep her 'secret', and became even more desperate to pay any price that the cure-all count demanded for his elixirs. His suave charm, irresistible bedside manner and touches of luxury – wrapping pills in gold leaf – all helped him get away with extortionate charges for herbal remedies any doctor could have prescribed.

As the Grand Cophta's fame spread, more and more countries demanded to see this man of magic powers for themselves. The nobles of the independent Baltic state of Courland were so impressed that they proposed crowning the count king. He wisely declined.

In Moscow, one of the Tsar's ministers urged Cagliostro to cure his insane brother. The count wanted to inspect the patient, who was brought before him, securely bound. Acting on the count's instructions, the Russians untied the madman, and he charged his would-be benefactor, threatening to kill him. The count knocked him aside, then had him thrown into an icy river. Amazingly, when pulled out, the man was sane and apologetic.

But it was after he moved to Strasbourg in 1780 that Count Cagliostro achieved his greatest fame. By this time, he was claiming to have been born before Noah's flood, to have studied under Socrates, to have talked with Moses, Solomon and Roman emperors, to have drunk wine at a wedding feast in Cana, Galilee. And he was dating his letters 550 B.C.

He was also still confidently dispensing potions which cured patients whom other doctors had given up as lost causes. The French government set up a commission of eminent medical men and scientists to investigate several unorthodox healers, and they pronounced many of Cagliostro's cures genuine, while admitting they could find no scientific explanation.

Soon his achievements came to the attention of the arrogant archbishop of the city, Prince Cardinal Louis de Rohan. A servant was sent to summon Cagliostro but returned alone with a message:

'If the prince is ill, let him come to me and I will cure him,' the count had said. 'If he is not ill, he has no need of me and I have no need of him.'

Such impudence was unheard of. But once de Rohan overcame his initial rage, he was intrigued enough to invent a minor ailment to justify visiting the man everyone was talking about. And so began the patronage that was to establish the count as one of Europe's most powerful men, and drag him down to despair.

When Cagliostro cured the Prince Cardinal's brother, Prince de Soubise, of scarlatina – something the greatest doctors of Paris had failed to do – adulation knew no bounds. The count's effigy began appearing on snuff boxes, shoe buckles, rings and medallions.

Then de Rohan overstepped himself. Anxious to ingratiate himself with Queen Marie Antoinette, with whom he had fallen out of favour, he hatched a bizarre plot to obtain a diamond necklace she wanted. When King Louis XVI learned he had been forging letters in the queen's name and disguising a woman as the queen, he had the Prince Cardinal arrested – and his protégés, the Cagliostros, were also thrown into the Bastille.

A public trial completely cleared them of involvement in the conspiracy, and nine months later they were escorted home in triumph by thousands of delighted supporters. But the damage had been done. Under intense interrogation, Lorenza had revealed too much about the tricks of Balsamo's trade. Slowly the truth about his money, his elixirs, his lifestyle began to emerge.

The furious Louis kicked the couple out of France, with dire warnings not to return. Again they wandered Europe, growing increasingly poor and shunned. Finally, Lorenza, tiring of her husband now that the glamour, riches and excitement had gone, persuaded him to return with her to Rome.

It was a crazy blunder – any Roman Catholic joining the Freemasons was subject to excommunication as a heretic. Yet Balsamo compounded his career by creating a new Egyptian Rite Masonic Lodge to try to revive his fortunes.

The papal police quickly seized him, and on April 7, 1791 he was found guilty of heresy and sentenced to die. Lorenza had denounced him, hoping to save herself. She was locked away in a convent for the rest of her life.

The Pope's mercy saved Balsamo for a while. The death sentence was commuted to life imprisonment in the dungeons of Italy's strongest fortress, San Leo. And there, on August 26, 1795, Count Alessandro di Cagliostro, the man who had proclaimed himself immortal, died, aged fifty-two.

The Pop Duo that Tricked the World

Milli Vanilli was a pop/dance music project formed by Frank Farian in Germany in 1988, fronted by Fab Morvan and Rob Pilatus. The group's debut album achieved high sales internationally which earned them a Grammy Award for Best New Artist on February 21, 1990. The act became one of the most popular pop acts in the late 1980s and early 1990s. However, their success turned to infamy when their Grammy was revoked after it was revealed that the lead vocals on the record were not the actual voices of Morvan and Pilatus. In 1998, ten years after Milli Vanilli's initial debut, Rob Pilatus was found dead in a Frankfurt hotel of an apparent drug overdose.

Beginnings

When Frank Farian developed the concept of Milli Vanilli, he chose to feature vocals by Charles Shaw, John Davis, Brad Howell, and twin sisters Jodie and Linda Rocco; however, he felt that those singers lacked a marketable image. He then recruited Robert Pilatus and Fabrice Morvan, two younger model/dancers he found dancing in a Munich dance club, to front the act. Milli Vanilli's debut album *All or Nothing* was released in Europe in mid-1988, with Rob and Fab's pictures on the front and center of the albums, but no mention of who actually sang the songs. The success of the record caught the attention of Arista Records who signed the duo. Arista deleted several tracks from the original album, added several new ones (including a new track written by Diane Warren, "Blame It on the Rain"), remixed many of the tracks and renamed the album to *Girl You Know It's True* for release in the American market in early 1989.

This version of the album went six times platinum and led to the rerelease of the title track, which peaked at number 2 on the Hot 100 in April of that year and was certified platinum.

(The song was a cover version of a Numarx track published in 1987 on the US Bluebird label.) The U.K. release featured the original first album and the remix album together as "2 X 2". Even greater commercial success followed, as the pair's next three singles "Baby Don't Forget My Number", "Girl I'm Gonna Miss You" and "Blame It on the Rain" all reached number 1. A fifth and final single "All or Nothing", also made the Top 5 in the beginning of 1990 in a remixed form which sampled the "Keep On Movin" beat from UK soul act Soul II Soul. Milli Vanilli's meteoric rise to pop music superstardom culminated with a Grammy Award for Best New Artist on February 22, 1990.

Media Backlash

The first sign that the group was lip-synching happened in late 1989 during a live performance on MTV at the Lake Compounce theme park in Bristol, Connecticut. As they performed onstage live in front of an audience, the recording of the song "Girl You Know It's True" jammed and began to skip, repeating the partial line "Girl, you know it's . . ." over and over on the speakers. They continued to pretend to sing and dance onstage for a few more moments, then they both ran offstage. According to the episode of VH1's *Behind the Music* which profiled Milli Vanilli, Downtown Julie Brown stated that fans attending the concert didn't seem to care or even notice and the concert continued as if nothing unusual had happened.

Unlike the international release of *All or Nothing*, the inserts for the American version clearly attributed the voices on the album to Morvan and Pilatus. This prompted Shaw to disclose to *New York Newsday* writer John Leland in December 1989 that he was one of three singers on Milli Vanilli's hit debut album, and that Pilatus and Morvan were impostors. Farian reportedly paid Shaw $150,000 to retract his statements, though this did not stem the tide of public criticism. Because of rising public questions regarding the source of who actually sang in the group, as well as the insistence of Morvan and Pilatus to Farian that they be allowed to sing on the next album, Farian confessed to reporters on November 12, 1990, that Morvan and Pilatus did not actually sing on the records. As a result of American media pressure, Milli Vanilli's Grammy was withdrawn four days later (however, their three American Music Awards were never withdrawn because the organisers felt the awards were given to them by music consumers), and Arista Records dropped the act from its roster and deleted their album and its masters from their catalogue, taking *Girl You Know It's True* out of print.

After these details emerged, at least twenty-six different lawsuits were filed under various U.S. consumer fraud protection laws against Pilatus, Morvan and Arista Records. One such filing occurred on November 22, 1990 in Ohio, where lawyers there filed a class action lawsuit asking for refunds on behalf of a local woman in Cuyahoga County who had bought *Girl You Know It's True*; at the time the lawsuit was filed, it was estimated at least 1,000 Ohio residents had bought the album. On August 12, 1991, a proposed settlement to a refund lawsuit in Chicago, Illinois was rejected. This settlement would have refunded buyers of Milli Vanilli CDs, cassettes, records, or singles. However, the refunds would only be given as a credit for a future Arista release. On August 28, a new settlement was approved; it refunded those who attended concerts along with those who bought Milli Vanilli recordings. An estimated 10 million buyers were eligible to claim a refund and they could keep the refunded recordings as well. The deadline to claim refunds passed on March 8, 1992.

The Real Milli Vanilli and Album *The Moment of Truth*

The material for Milli Vanilli's second album had been recorded and finalised in Spring 1990. In the autumn, the first single "Keep on Running" was released for radio play, shortly before Farian revealed the truth about Milli Vanilli. At the last minute, Farian had the artwork to the second Milli Vanilli album changed to depict the actual singers instead of Morvan and Pilatus, changed the album's title from *Keep on Running* (the name had been meant to correspond with the first single), and changed the artist name to The Real Milli Vanilli. However, the graphic artist who performed the change forgot to update the album cover's spine, so the second album still had the original artist and album name on the spine ("Milli Vanilli — Keep On Running").

The resulting album, released in Europe in early 1991, was renamed *The Moment of Truth* and spawned three singles, "Keep On Running," "Nice 'n Easy" and "Too Late (True Love)." A Morvan/Pilatus lookalike named Ray Horton was depicted on the cover and provided vocals on four tracks. In addition, the album featured rappers Icy Bro on "Hard As Hell" and Tammy T on "Too Late (True Love)." A Diane Warren penned song, "When I Die," has been covered by several other artists, including Farian's "No Mercy." For the American market, Farian chose to avoid any association to Milli Vanilli and had the tracks rerecorded with Ray Horton on the majority of lead vocals.

Try 'N' B

In 1992, RCA signed onto release the album as the debut of the newly created group Try 'N' B. The self-titled release included three additional tracks not on The Real Milli Vanilli release: "Ding Dong," "Who Do You Love," and a remake of Dr. Hook's "Sexy Eyes." Because of significantly better sales under the name Try 'N' B in America, a slightly modified Try 'N' B debut album was released internationally.

Album *Rob & Fab*

Meanwhile, Morvan and Pilatus moved to Los Angeles, California, and signed to the Joss Entertainment Group, where they recorded their followup album under the name *Rob & Fab*. Almost all the songs on the album were written by Kenny Taylor and Fabrice Morvan, while Morvan and Pilatus provided the lead vocals. Because of financial constraints, Joss Entertainment Group was only able to release the album in the United States, the most critical of all markets to Milli Vanilli. A single, "We Can Get It On", was made available for radio play shortly before the album's release. However, the lack of publicity, poor distribution and the scandal surrounding Milli Vanilli's lip-synching allegations led to its failure.

Milli Vanilli Comeback and Death of Rob Pilatus

In order to restore their career, Farian agreed in 1997 to produce a new Milli Vanilli album with Morvan and Pilatus on lead vocals. This all led up to the recording of the 1998 Milli Vanilli comeback album *Back and in Attack*. Even some of the original studio singers backed the performers in their attempt to bring back some of the fame that had been shed so quickly. However, Rob Pilatus encountered a number of personal problems during the production of the new album. He turned to drugs and crime, committing a series of robberies and ultimately serving three months in jail in California. Farian paid for Pilatus to attend six months of drug rehabilitation and plane tickets for him to fly back to Germany. On the eve of the new album's promotional tour on April 2, 1998, Pilatus was found dead of a suspected alcohol and prescription pill overdose in a Frankfurt hotel room. Pilatus' death was ruled accidental.

Fab Morvan's Solo Career

Morvan spent the following years as a session musician and public speaker while working on his musical abilities. In 1998, he was a DJ at famed L.A. radio station KIIS-FM. During this time, he also performed at the station's sold-out 1999 Wango Tango festival concert before 50,000 people at Dodger Stadium.

Morvan then spent 2001 on tour before performing in 2002 as the inaugural performer at the brand-new Velvet Lounge at the Hard Rock Café Hotel in Orlando, Florida. In 2003, Morvan released his first solo album, *Love Revolution*. He marketed the album through his website and CD Baby. Morvan's songs "Roll" and "Time Will Reveal" can be heard on his MySpace profile page.

✿✿

The Greatest Art Forger in the World

As dawn broke on October 29, 1947, there was already a line of would-be spectators outside the Fourth Chamber of the District Court in Amsterdam's Prinsengracht.

By the time the court sat at ten o'clock, the courtroom was filled with two hundred onlookers, swelled by press representatives from all over the world who had come to see the trial of the man who can claim to be the greatest art forger of all time.

The man in question was a fifty-eight-year-old artist and confirmed morphia addict, who suffered from angina. Dressed in a pale blue shirt, dark blue tie, and an elegant dark blue suit—but looking gaunt and hollow-cheeked—he did his best to exude an air of jaunty confidence, waving to his friends, his son and daughter and his divorced second wife Jo, as he entered the court.

Round the walls hung some of the pictures he was alleged to have forged—*Christ at Emmaus, Head of Christ, The Last Supper,* and *Isaac Blessing Jacob*, all of which were attributed to the great seventeenth-century Dutch artist Vermeer—although, in fact, the signatures on the canvases had all been cleverly faked, as had the entire paintings, by the man in the dock.

As soon as the presiding judge had taken his seat on the bench, the clerk of the court asked the prisoner: "Are you Henricus Antonius van Meegeren?" The clerk used the Latin style of nomenclature which was customary on formal occasions, although the prisoner's two first names were often contracted to Han, by which he was generally known.

The defendant acknowledged his identity with a curt nod, after which the Public Prosecutor read the indictment. The defendant was charged under two counts – first, that he had obtained money by fraud, and secondly, that he had put false names or signatures "on certain paintings" contrary to Articles 326 and 326 B of the Netherlands Penal Code.

"Accused, do you admit the charges?" the judge addressed the man in the dock.

"I do," answered van Meegeren.

The fact that Han van Meegeren was in the dock at all had been the result of a chance happening two years previously, when the Allied Military Government Art Commission had discovered a large collection of pictures in a disused salt mine near Salzburg. The pictures had been mostly looted by the Nazis from museums and private collections in Europe.

It was the task of the Commission to return such finds to their owners, and also to seek out and punish "collaborators" who were known to have disposed them of. One of the pictures found in the salt mine was listed as *Christ with the Woman Taken in Adultery* and bore the prominent Vermeer signature – the usual "I.V.MEER" in the top left-hand corner.

accompanying particulars revealed this painting belonged to Field Marshal Goering, who had acquired it from a Bavarian banker named Aloys Miedl, who had an office in Amsterdam.

Although the price was the absurdly large one of 1,650,000 guilders—the equivalent of half a million pounds or, one and a quarter million dollars—Goering had not paid in cash but in kind, and had handed over in exchange for the *Woman Taken in Adultery* more than two hundred paintings which had been stolen from Holland by the occupying Nazis.

Further inquiries showed that Miedl had got the picture from an intermediary called Dr. Hofer, who made a business of supplying leading Nazis with art treasures for their own collections. And that Hofer had in turn got it from a Dutch art dealer timed Rienstra van Strijvesande, to whom it had been entrusted by van Meegeren to sell on commission and whom the authorities later failed to trace.

When two uniformed officers of the Netherlands Field Security Service called at van Meegeren's large house on the Keizergracht one day in May 1945, and told him they were investigating the circumstances of the sale of an important painting by Vermeer, van Meegeren received a shock.

He admitted that he had sold the *Woman Taken in Adultery* to van Strijvesande during the war, but that the dealer had assured him that it would not fall into any German hands.

The security men were prepared to accept this explanation. But they told van Meegeren that in view of the work's undoubted importance, the high price paid for it, and the identity of the buyer, they would have to know where he had obtained it. Such information, they assured him, would be treated as strictly confidential.

However, all van Meegeren would tell them was that he had bought the picture from "an old Italian family" who had fallen on hard times and been forced to sell their family treasures.

Van Meegeren's choice of an Italian background for the painting may have made the authorities suspect—quite wrongly—that he had been acting as a middleman between the Fascists and the Nazis for the disposal of looted works of art.

At all events, he was arrested four days later and charged with being a collaborator.

"No Great Treasure"

For the next six weeks Han van Meegeren persisted in his refusal to supply any further information about the picture. Then, perhaps because he was depressed and suffering from the effect of the lack of his accustomed drugs, he broke down before his astonished interrogators.

"You are fools like the rest of them!" he exclaimed. "I sold no great national treasure, and painted it myself!"

If he had stopped there, all might have been well and no doubt he would have been lauded as a wartime hero who had duped the Nazis. But his innate conceit made him go on and declare that he had likewise painted three more supposed Vermeers and a de Hoogh—*Christ at Emmaus, Head of Christ, The Washing of Christ's Feet*, all signed "I.V.Meer", and *Interior with Drinkers,* signed "P.D.H.1658" and ascribed to de Hoogh.

The latter painting, like *Christ at Emmaus*, had been bought by Dr. D. G. van Beuningen, a well-known private collector in Rotterdam. At the time it was remarked that it bore a strong resemblance to de Hoogh's undoubted work *The Cardplayers*, which is in the Royal Collection at Buckingham Palace.

For *Christ at Emmaus*, which was the first of van Meegeren's forgeries to come on the market—at Rotterdam in 1937—and was later presented to the city's Boymans Museum, van Beuningen paid the equivalent of £180,000 or $450,000. At the time it was hailed by the eminent art historian Dr. Abraham Bredius as the most important example of the work of Jan Vermeer of Delft.

At first the police thought that van Meegeren was either mad or else had invented a farfetched story in order to escape conviction on a more serious charge. They began to change their minds when they subjected the *Woman Taken in Adultery* to an X-ray test, which revealed that it had been painted over an earlier picture on a genuine old canvas as van Meegeren told them he had done.

The police then put it to van Meegeren that, if he had really painted *Christ at Emmaus*, he should be able to make a copy without much difficulty. Since this was within the capability of any skilled artist, van Meegeren dismissed such a naive proposal with contempt.

Instead, he made the police an alternative proposal, namely that he should be given his freedom and allowed to work in his studio with the materials, including drugs, that he needed. He would then create another Vermeer before their eyes.

This novel proposal was agreed to and van Meegeren accordingly set to work on a large canvas, 58 ¾ x 75 ½ inches, to produce the work known as *Young Christ Teaching in the Temple.*

Although two members of the security police were always present in the studio, and he painted under some difficulty, nevertheless he finished his last "masterpiece" in two months.

The authorities now dropped the accusation of collaboration with the wartime enemy, and substituted charges of fraud and forgery. At the same time, the Minister of Justice appointed a commission of experts—led by Dr. P. B. Coremans, Director of the Central Laboratory of Belgian Museums—to pronounce upon the eight supposed forgeries.

The experts, consisting of two art historians and three scientists, were the principal witnesses for the prosecution when, after considerable delay, the case came to trial. Indeed they found the defendant artist most cooperative since he supplied them with all the details of his technique and the materials he had used.

Each member of the Coremans Commission was asked two questions at the trial—whether in his opinion all the paintings were modern and whether they could be the work of van Meegeren. All replied to both questions in the affirmative.

Then the curtains in court were drawn and Dr. Coremans showed with the aid of slides how these conclusions had been reached.

There was the "crackle" in the paint, the cross sections of the layers, the presence of artificial resin, and finally a fragment of the original canvas on which he had overpainted *Christ at Emmaus*, mounted on its original wooden stretcher, and from which van Meegeren had cut a vertical strip 30 to 50 centimeters wide.

Sawn-off Pieces

He had shortened the horizontal arms of the stretcher by the same amount, and he had left the sawn-off pieces together with the strip of canvas at the Villa Primavera in Rocquebrune, where he had painted *Christ at Emmaus*.

Asked for his comment on the defendant's work when he had finished his lecture, Dr. Coremans said: "I find this work excellent. Indeed it is phenomenal. It will never be possible to get away with forgery again."

The next witness was another member of the Commission, Dr. A. M. de Wild, who had advised the Netherlands government to buy the least good of van Meegeren's pseudo-Vermeers, *The Washing of Christ's Feet*—which it had done in 1943 for 1,300,000 guilders (about £320,000 or $800,000). Since the witness had subsequently served on the Commission which declared it to be false, he was asked to explain the apparent discrepancy.

Dr. de Wild tried to excuse himself by saying that the dealer with whom he had negotiated twice refused to allow the picture to be X-rayed. "Later on I was able to do so myself," he said. "This brought about my change of opinion."

When the pompous Dr. de Wild went so far as to claim personal credit, the court laughed outright. "It soon became clear to me that the accused had borrowed a formula for the composition of his quasi-old paints from my treatise on the methods of Vermeer and de Hoogh," he declared.

When the experts had finished their testimony, the judge leaned forward and asked the defendant at what stage in each work he had added the signature.

"I did that last of all and it was much the hardest job," replied van Meegeren with a sigh, as he remembered just how difficult the operation was. "It had to be done in a single stroke. Once I had begun it, there could be no going back."

The next witness was a house agent named Strijbis, who had acted as agent for van Meegeren in disposing of his fakes. "I was already acquainted with the accused when he asked me, in 1941, if I would sell a painting for him," he stated in answer to the Public Prosecutor. "I knew nothing about art but he offered me a handsome commission—one sixth of whatever price I got. I took the work, a *Head of Christ*, to Hoogendijk."

Hoogendijk was the leading Amsterdam art dealer at that time, and had been concerned with the negotiations for the sale of *Christ at Emmaus*.

"Did you know it was a fake?" the Public Prosecutor rapped out the question.

"Certainly not," protested the witness. "The accused said it was a Vermeer. He never told me where he obtained it. Later I sold three others for him, all to Hoogendijk: *the Last Supper*, a Pieter de Hoogh and the *Blessing of Jacob*. They were supposed to be all from the same collection."

"What were the prices paid?"

"I no longer remember," replied Strijbis. "I kept no records of them."

In fact the total money paid for the four forgeries sold by Strijbis was about 3 ½ million guilders, of which his share was more than half a million—on which sum he had paid no tax.

The next witness was the dealer himself. "I walked into the trap," Hoogendijk admitted. "When I saw the *Head of Christ*, it made me think of the *Emmaus*."

"Did you not think it strange that more and more Vermeers were being discovered?" the Public Prosecutor asked.

"No," replied Hoogendijk. "The art historians agree that there should be more, that the *Emmaus* could not be the only one of its kind. I sold the *Head of Christ* to Dr. van Beuningen. That was in 1941, in Rotterdam. It was a much finer painting then than it is now."

Asked how he accounted for the acceptance of the *Blessing of Jacob*, he turned to have another look at it on the wall of the courtroom before replying.

"Yes, it's difficult to explain," he said after studying the painting for a minute or two. "It is unbelievable that it fooled me. But we all slid downwards—from the *Emmaus* to the *Last Supper*, from the *Last Supper* to the *Blessing of Jacob*. When I look at them now, I don't understand how it could possibly have happened.

"A psychologist could explain it better than I can. But it should be remembered that the wartime atmosphere contributed to our blindness, and in particular the *Emmaus* had been declared authentic by experts of world-wide reputation. There was also the desire to keep the paintings in Holland."

In fact a psychologist, or properly speaking a psychiatrist, did take the stand, and testified in professional jargon. "The character of the defendant leads to sensitiveness to criticism, fed by a revenge complex which explains his antisocial attitude," he stated. "I would describe him as disequilibrated but fully responsible for his actions."

The psychiatrist went on to say that in his opinion a man of van Meegeren's personality "would be greatly hurt by being kept in isolation," and he would not advise a prison sentence.

Dr. Hannema, the Director of the Boymans Museum, was then called to the witness stand. He described how *The Washing of Christ's Feet* had been bought by the government, though it was never hung.

"I immediately got the impression that it was a Vermeer," he added. "It was examined by a government committee which decided to advise its purchase. None of us liked it much, but we were afraid it would go to Germany.

The museum director was followed on the stand by Dr. van Beuningen. He said he had always been convinced of the authenticity of his three purchases, the two Vermeers and the de Hoogh. "I never had any doubts," he declared.

When the evidence was concluded, the presiding judge asked the man in the dock. "You still admit that you painted all these fakes?"

"Yes, Mr. President," answered van Meegeren.

"And also that you sold them, at a very high price?"

"I had no alternative. If I had sold them at a low price, it would have been an indication that they were false."

"Why did you continue after the *Emmaus*?" the judge persisted.

"I found the process so beautiful," van Meegeren replied blandly. "I came to a condition in which I was no longer my own master. I became without will, powerless. I was forced to continue."

"Perhaps the financial side had some influence on your actions?"

"It made little difference," answered van Meegeren. "The millions I earned from the later pictures were added to the millions I had earned already. I didn't do it for the money, which brought me nothing but trouble and unhappiness."

"So you acted from no desire for financial gain?"

"Only from a desire to paint. I decided to carry on, not primarily from a desire to paint forgeries but to make the best use of the technique I had developed. I intend to continue using that technique. It's an excellent one. But I will never again offer my paintings as old masters'."

Considerable Sympathy

In his closing speech the Public Prosecutor, who was well aware of the considerable public sympathy expressed for van Meegeren for having so successfully fooled the art world, did not press the case against the defendant with any noticeable enthusiasm. He asked for a two-year prison sentence, half the maximum possible.

It was then the turn of Meester Heldring, van Meegeren's defence counsel. His speech was witty and persuasive and all times anecdotal. For instance, he told how his client visited the Boymans Museum in 1938 to view the acquisition of the latest Vermeer and was reproved by the attendant on duty for coming too close to it.

Counsel went on to analyse each of the sales and argued that in none of them was there any fraud or false pretence.

It had never been said (except possibly to Strijbis) that a canvas was a Vermeer or a de Hoogh, or even that it might be —in each case this had been left to the expert or the dealer or the buyer.

On the fraud charge Meester Heldring submitted that his client was not guilty and asked for an acquittal. On the forgery charge he asked the court to exercise the "utmost leniency".

Asked by the presiding judge whether he had anything to say, van Meegeren replied "No". The court then adjourned for two weeks to consider its verdict, and van Meegeren, who had been granted bail, went home.

On November 12, he was brought up again to hear the judge's verdict: guilty on both counts, for which he was sentenced to one year in prison, the minimum possible.

The Court also ordered that the forged paintings should be returned to their owners, with the exception of *The Young Christ* which van Meegeren had painted at the instigation of the police. This was to be sold for the benefit of his creditors in his bankruptcy.

Van Meegeren's counsel drafted a petition for a free pardon which was forwarded to Queen Wilhelmina. Since the Public Prosecutor stated that he would not oppose it, there is little doubt that it would have been granted if the master forger had lived. But before the Queen's decision could be announced, van Meegeren suffered a fatal heart attack.

He died at the Valerium Clinic in Amsterdam on December 29, 1947—his belief in his talent as a painter of originality and genius undiminished.

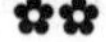

Yellow Kid

Joseph "Yellow Kid" Weil (Born: 1877; Died: 1975) was one of the most famous con men in his era. Over the course of his career he is believed to have stolen over 8 million dollars. In his first job as a collector, he realised that his co-workers were collecting their debts but keeping a little part of the money for themselves. Weil started a protection racket – offering not to report their activities in return for a small portion of what they were taking.

He also used phony oil deals, women, fixed races, and an endless list of other tricks to steal from an increasingly gullible public. He could change his persona daily to further his gains: one day he was Dr. Henri Reuel, a noted geologist who travelled around and told his hosts that he was a representative for a big oil company while draining them of the cash they gave him to "invest in fuel." The next day he was director of the Elysium Development Company, promising land to innocent believers while robbing them in recording and abstract fees. Or he was a chemist par excellence, who had discovered how to copy dollar bills; promising to increase your fortune, he would multiply your bill's then take the booty once the police arrived.

In his autobiography, Weil writes:

"The desire to get something for nothing has been very costly to many people who have dealt with me and with other con men," Weil writes. "But I have found that this is the way it works. The average person, in my estimation, is ninety-nine percent animal and one percent human. The ninety-nine percent that is animal causes very little trouble. But the one percent that is human causes all our woes. When people learn — as I doubt they will — that they can't get something for nothing, crime will diminish and we shall live in greater harmony."

✿✿

Sure Thing or Bunco Man

Soapy Smith (Born: 1860; Died: 1898) (born Jefferson Randolph Smith) was an American con artist and gangster who had a major hand in the organised criminal operations of Denver, Creede, Colorado, and Skagway, Alaska from 1879 to 1898. He is perhaps the most famous "sure-thing" bunko man of the old west. Some time in the late 1870s or early 1880s, Smith began duping entire crowds with a ploy the Denver newspapers dubbed 'The Prize Package Soap Sell Swindle'.

Jefferson would open his "tripe and keister" (display case on a tripod) on a busy street corner. Piling ordinary soap cakes onto the keister top, he would describe their wonders. As he spoke to the growing crowd of curious onlookers, he would pull out his wallet and begin wrapping paper money ranging from one dollar up to one hundred dollars, around a select few of the bars. He then finished each bar by wrapping plain paper around it to hide the money. He mixed the money-wrapped packages in with wrapped bars containing no money. He then sold the soap to the crowd for a dollar a cake.

A shill planted in the crowd would buy a bar, tear it, open it, and loudly proclaim that he had won some money,

waving it around for all to see. This performance had the desired effect of enticing the sale of the packages. More often than not, victims bought several bars before the sale was completed. Midway through the sale, Smith would announce that the hundred-dollar bill still remained in the pile, unpurchased. He then would auction off the remaining soap bars to the highest bidders.

Through the masterful art of manipulation and sleight-of-hand, the cakes of soap wrapped with money were hidden and replaced with packages holding no cash. It was assured that the only money "won" went to members of what became known as the "Soap Gang." Soapy was eventually shot to death by a group he swindled in a card game.

Phony M15 Agent

Robert Hendy-Freegard (Born: 1971) is a British barman, car salesman, con man and impostor who masqueraded as an MI5 agent and fooled several people to go underground for fear of IRA assassination. He met his victims on social occasions or as customers in the pub or car dealership where he was working. He would reveal his "role" as an undercover agent for MI5, Special Branch or Scotland Yard working against the IRA.

He would win them over, ask for money and make them do his bidding. He demanded that they cut off contact with family and friends, go through "loyalty tests" and live alone in poor conditions. He seduced five women, claiming that he wanted to marry them. Initially some of the victims refused to cooperate with the police because he had warned them that police would be double agents or MI5 agents performing another "loyalty test".

Hendy-Freegard also seduced a newly married personal assistant who was taking care of his children. He told her he was with MI5 and forced her to cut contact with friends and family lest the IRA would kill her. He also took naked pictures of her and threatened to give them to her husband if she would not cooperate. She had to change her name and tell the deed poll officer it was because she was sexually abused as a child. Her loyalty tests included sleeping in Heathrow airport and on park benches for several nights and pretending to be a Jehovah's witness so that his bosses in MI5 would let them marry.

In 2002 Scotland Yard and the FBI organised a sting operation. First, the FBI bugged the phone of the American psychologist's parents. Her mother told Hendy-Freegard she would hand over £10,000 but only in person. Hendy-Freegard met the mother in Heathrow airport where police apprehended him. He denied all charges and claimed they were part of a conspiracy against him and continued this story in the subsequent trial. On June 23, 2005, after an eight month trial, Blackfriars Crown Court convicted Robert Hendy-Freegard for two counts of kidnapping, 10 of theft and 8 of deception. On September 6, 2005 he was given a life sentence. Police doubt that they have discovered all the victims. On April 25, 2007, the BBC reported that Robert Hendy-Freegard had appealed against his kidnapping convictions and won. This means that the life sentence is revoked but he will still serve nine years for the other offences. He could be free by the end of 2007.

✿✿

Bernard Cornfeld

Bernard Cornfeld (Born: 1927; Died: 1995) was a prominent businessman and international financier who sold investments in US mutual funds. He was born in Turkey. When he moved to the US, he first worked as a social worker but became a mutual fund salesman in the 1950s. Although he suffered from a stammer, he had a natural gift for selling and when a schoolfriend's father died, the two of them used the $3,000 insurance money to purchase and run an age and weight guessing stand at the Coney Island funfair.

In the 1960s, Cornfeld formed his own mutual fund selling company, Investors Overseas Services (IOS), which he incorporated outside the US with funds in Canada and headquarters in Geneva, Switzerland. Although the headquarters were officially in Geneva, the main operational offices of IOS were in Ferney-Voltaire, France, a short drive from the Swiss border to Geneva—this was simply a means of avoiding the problems of obtaining Swiss work-permits for the many employees. During the next ten years, IOS raised in excess of $2.5 billion, bringing Cornfeld a personal fortune of more than $100 million. Cornfeld himself became known for conspicuous consumption with lavish parties. Socially, he was generous and jovial.

A group of 300 IOS employees complained to the Swiss authorities that Cornfeld and his co-founders pocketed part of the proceeds of a share issue raised among employees in 1969. Consequently he was charged with fraud in 1973 by the Swiss authorities. When Cornfeld visited Geneva, Swiss authorities arrested him. He served eleven months in a Swiss jail before being freed on a bail surety of $600,000. He returned to Beverly Hills, living less ostentatiously than in his previous years. He developed an obsession for health foods and vitamins, renounced red meat and seldom drank alcohol. He suffered a stroke and died of a cerebral aneurysm on February 27, 1995 in London, England.

✿✿

Nurse of George Washington

Joice Heth was an elderly black woman whom a young P.T. Barnum put on display in 1835, advertising that she was the 161 year old former nurse of George Washington. Heth entertained audiences with tales about the young George Washington, and her exhibition drew substantial attention.

When the public's interest in her waned, Barnum rekindled its curiosity by spreading a rumour that Joice Heth was actually not a person at all, but instead was a mechanical automaton. People then revisited the exhibit to determine for themselves whether she was an automaton or a real person. Barnum displayed her until February 19, 1836, on which day she died.

However, even in death Barnum continued to use her to

draw crowds. He allowed a public autopsy to be performed on her body for the purpose of verifying her age. Unfortunately for Barnum, the doctor who performed the autopsy declared that she could not have been older than eighty. Barnum struck back by planting a story in the New York Herald (February 27, 1836) explaining that the body that had been autopsied had not actually been the body of Joice Heth.

THE GREATEST

Natural & National

CURIOSITY

IN THE WORLD.

Nurse to Gen. GEORGE WASHINGTON, (the Father of our country,)
WILL BE SEEN AT

Barnum's Hotel, Bridgeport,

On FRIDAY, and SATURDAY, the 11th & 12th days
of December, DAY AND EVENING.

JOICE HETH is unquestionably the most astonishing and interesting curiosity in the World! She was the slave of Augustine Washington, (the father of Gen. Washington,) and was the first person who put clothes on the unconscious infant, who, in after days, led our heroic fathers onto glory, to victory, and freedom. To use her own language when speaking of the illustrious Father of his Country, "she raised him." JOICE HETH was born in the year 1674, and has consequently, now arrived at the astonishing

AGE OF 161 YEARS.

Barnum's collaborator in the scheme, Levi Lyman, later added another chapter to the saga by supplying the Herald with what he claimed was the real Joice Heth story. This ran in the Herald beginning on September 8, 1836 in a series of six articles. In this article, Lyman claimed that Barnum had discovered the elderly black woman on a plantation and had taught her to pretend she had been George Washington's nurse. But again, this story was also false. The truth was that Barnum had not found Heth on his own. Instead, he had simply bought the rights to exhibit Joice Heth from someone else who was already exhibiting her, and that he had never coached her.

Gregor MacGregor: Chief of Poyais

Gregor MacGregor was a Scottish soldier, adventurer and coloniser who fought in the South American struggle for independence. Upon his return to England in 1820, he claimed to be *cacique* of Poyais (also known as *Principality of Poyais, Territory of Poyais, Republic of Poyais*). Poyais was a fictional Central American country that MacGregor had invented which, with his help, drew investors and eventually colonists.

Early Life

MacGregor was born in Edinburgh, Scotland on Christmas Eve 1786. His parents were Captain Daniel MacGregor and Ann Austin.

In 1803, he joined the Royal Navy. He married Marie Bowater in 1805, who died soon after. He then served in the Spanish and Portuguese armies, after which he returned to Edinburgh.

By this time, MacGregor heard about the independence movements in South America and in the Captaincy General of Venezuela in particular, where he arrived in 1811 with the rank of Colonel.

Green Cross of Florida

In 1817, MacGregor led a group of 55 men to capture San Fernandina on Amelia Island, Florida from the Spanish. Surprising the Spanish, MacGregor's men overran the island on June 29. MacGregor raised a flag with a green cross on it. He left a few months later to fight the Spanish.

Cacique of Poyais

Gregor MacGregor went from Latin America to London, England, in 1820 and pronounced that he had been created *cacique* (highest authority or prince) of the Principality of

Poyais, an independent nation on the Bay of Honduras. Native chief King George Frederic Augustus I of the Mosquito Shore and Nation had given him the territory of Poyais, 12,500 mile^2 (32,400 km^2) of fertile land with untapped resources, a small number of settlers of British origin, and cooperative natives eager to please. He had created the beginnings of a country with civil service, army and democratic government. Now he needed settlers and investment and had come back to the United Kingdom to give people the opportunity.

At the time, British merchants were all too eager to enter the South American market that Spain had denied to them. The region had already become more promising in the wake of wars of South American independence, when the new governments of Colombia, Chile and Peru had issued bonds in London Royal Exchange to raise money.

London high society welcomed the colourful figure of MacGregor, and he and his Spanish American wife Josefa Andrea Lovera received many invitations. The Lord Mayor of London Christopher Magnay even organised an official reception in London Guildhall. MacGregor claimed descent of clan MacGregor and that Rob Roy MacGregor had been his direct ancestor. He enhanced his allure by telling about his exploits in the Peninsular War and later in the service of Francisco de Miranda, Simón Bolívar and South American independence — tales which were rather embellished.

MacGregor was also introduced to Major William John Richardson and by the winter of 1821 he had made Richardson legate of Poyais. He had also moved to Oak Hall in Richardson's estate in Essex, England, as befit his station as a prince. An office for the Legation of the Territory of Poyais was opened at Dowgate Hill in the City of London. MacGregor enhanced his popularity with elaborate banquets in Oak Hall and invited dignitaries like foreign ambassadors, government ministers and senior military officers.

MacGregor also claimed that one of his ancestors was a rare survivor of the Darien Scheme, a failed Scottish attempt of colonisation in Panama in 1690s. In order to compensate for this, he said, he had decided to draw most of the settlers from Scotland. For this purpose, he established offices in Edinburgh and Glasgow.

In Edinburgh, MacGregor began to sell land rights for 3 shillings and 3 pence per acre (£0.16/acre or £40.15/km^2). The average worker's weekly wage at the time was about £1, which meant that the price was very generous. The price steadily rose to 4 shillings (£0.20). Many people willing to have a new start in the new land signed on with their families. On October 23, 1822 MacGregor raised a loan with the total of £200,000 on behalf of the Poyais government. It was in the form of 2,000 bearer bonds worth £100 each.

Also in 1822 MacGregor published a 350-page guidebook entitled *Sketch of the Mosquito Shore, including the Territory of Poyais, descriptive of the country*, supposedly written by one Captain Thomas Strangeways. It described the Poyais with glowing terms and mainly concentrated on how much profit one could get from the country's ample resources. Poyais was said to be a very anglophilic region with already existing infrastructure, untapped gold and silver mines and large amounts of fertile soil ready to be settled. The region was even free of tropical diseases. The book also claimed that British settlers had founded the capital of Poyais, St Joseph, in the 1730s.

Eager settlers

The Legation of Poyais chartered a ship called *Honduras Packet*, whose crew MacGregor already knew, and five London merchants received contracts to provision the ship with food and ammunition. Its cargo also included a chest full of "Poyais Dollars", Poyaisian currency MacGregor had printed in Scotland. Many of the settlers had changed their pounds to Poyais dollars.

On September 10, 1822 the *Honduras Packet* departed from the Port of London with 70 would-be-settlers aboard. They included doctors, lawyers and a banker who had been promised appropriate positions in the Poyais civil service. Some had also purchased officer commissions in the Poyaisian army.

On January 22, 1823 another ship, the *Kennersley Castle*, left Leith Harbour in Scotland for Poyais with 200 would-be-settlers. The ship also carried enough provisions for a year. It arrived in the appropriate place on March 20 and spent two days looking for a port. Eventually the newcomers found the settlers who had sailed on the *Honduras Packet*.

What the settlers had found was an untouched jungle, some natives and a couple of American hermits who had made their homes there. "St. Joseph" consisted only a couple of ruins of a previous attempt at settlement abandoned in the previous century. There was no settlement of any kind. The *Honduras Packet* had been swept away by a storm.

When some of the labourers began to build rudimentary shelter for themselves, the officers and civil servants decided to try to find a way out. Lieutenant Colonel Hector Hall, would-be governor of Poyais, had left to look for the *Honduras Packet* or another ship to take them back to Britain.

The would-be settlers began to argue with each other and some of them, who had expected better accommodation, refused to do anything. The *Kennersley Castle* sailed away. Tropical diseases also began to take their toll. One settler, having used his lifesavings to gain passage, committed suicide.

In April, the *Mexican Eagle*, an official ship from British Honduras with the chief magistrate on board, accidentally found the settlers. Chief magistrate Bennet listened to their story and told them that there was no such place as Poyais. He agreed to take them to British Honduras. A couple of days later Colonel Hall returned with King George Frederic and announced that the King had effectively revoked the land grant because MacGregor had assumed sovereignty. The *Mexican Eagle* took sixty settlers to British Honduras. The other settlers were rescued later.

Many settlers were weakened on their short sea voyage and many of them later died in hospitals in British Honduras. 180 of the 240 would-be settlers had perished during the ordeal.

Edward Codd, Superintendent for Belize, sent a warning to London where naval vessels were sent to call back five ships of would-be settlers that had departed after the *Kennersley Castle*. Those survivors who did not decide to settle on the British Honduras or move elsewhere in the Americas sailed on the *Ocean* on August 1, 1823 to London. More people died during that journey, and fewer than 50 came back alive to Britain.

Seventy-two days later the *Ocean* docked in London. The next day, city papers published the whole story.

However, regardless of the experiences of the survivors, some of them refused to believe that MacGregor would have been the main culprit. One of them, James Hastie, who had lost two of his children to tropical diseases, wrote and published a book *Narrative of a Voyage in the Ship Kennersley Castle from Leith Roads to Poyais*. He blamed Sir Gregor's advisers and publicists for spreading the false information. A group of survivors signed a declaration of their belief that had Sir Gregor gone with them, things would have turned out differently. Major Richardson sued the papers for libel and defended MacGregor against the charges of fraud.

MacGregor himself, however, had already left for Paris, France, in October.

Poyaisian Scheme in France

MacGregor had already contacted the trading organisation "Compagnie de la Nouvelle Neustrie" and commissioned it to further the affairs of Poyais in France.

In March 1825, MacGregor summoned from London Gustavus Butler Hippisley, an acquaintance from the army, on the pretext of discussing his appointment as a representative of Poyais in Colombia. Hippisley was to write about the Poyais affair in France in *Acts of Oppression Committed under the Administration of m. de Villele, Prime Minister of Charles X, in the years 1825-6*.

MacGregor claimed to Hippisley that he needed the help of the French government to obtain a formal renunciation of any (in reality nonexistent) claims Spain might have to Poyais and that he had met with French Prime Minister Jean-Baptiste de Villèle. MacGregor and la Nouvelle Noustrie already had plans to send French emigrants to Poyais. Hippisley wrote back to London, castigating the journalists who had called MacGregor a "penniless adventurer".

In August, MacGregor published a new constitution of Poyais; he had changed it into a republic with himself as the head of state. On August 18, 1825 he issued a £300.000 loan with 2.5% interest through the London bank of Thomas Jenkins & Company. The bond was probably never issued. At the same time, la Nouvelle Noustrie recruited settlers with the requirement that they buy FFr100 worth of the company shares.

When French officials noticed that a number of people had obtained passports in order to voyage to a country they had never heard of, they seized the la Nouvelle Neustrie vessel in Le Havre. Some of the would-be emigrants realised that something was not right and demanded investigation of the affairs of the la Nouvelle Neustrie and Sir Gregor. Hippisley was arrested but MacGregor was nowhere to be found.

Hippisley and MacGregor's secretary Thomas Irving were held in custody in La Force prison when the police investigation was going on. Lehuby, one of the directors of La Nouvelle Noustrie fled to Belgium. MacGregor went into hiding until he was brought into the prison December 7, two months after the first arrests. He proceeded to comfort his associates and in January 1826 made a proclamation to Central American states — it was written in French and primarily meant to affect French opinion. The accused were later moved to Bicetre prison.

The trial began on April 6, 1826. MacGregor, Hippisley, Irving and Lehuby (in absentia) were accused of fraud by means of the Poyais emigration program. Their lawyer, Merilhou, put the blame on Lehuby and the prosecutor was ready to withdraw the charges if the men were deported from France. Initially the court agreed but judges changed their minds when Belgium agreed to extradite Lehuby. Lawyer Merilhou was later summoned as a witness for the prosecution.

The new trial began on July 10, 1826, and lasted for four days. Merilhou's replacement, Berville, eloquently put the blame on anybody else but MacGregor. MacGregor was acquitted and Hippisley and Irving were released. Lehuby was convicted for 13 months for making false promises.

Lesser Poyais Schemes

In 1826 MacGregor returned to London, where the furor over his affairs had died down. Shortly after his arrival he was arrested and taken to Tothill Fields Bridewell prison in Westminster on charges now unknown. He was released in less than a week.

MacGregor proceeded with the modified schemes. This time he claimed that (again, nonexistent) natives had elected him as the head of state and became just "Cacigue of the Republic of Poyais" and opened a new office at 23 Threadneedle Street in the City, without any diplomatic trappings and in much a smaller scale than before. He issued a loan worth £800.000 as twenty year bonds with Thomas Jenkins & Company as brokers. The scheme was announced in the summer 1827.

However, investors were now more careful and somebody circulated a handbill that warned against investing in "Poyais humbug". MacGregor had to pass the most of the unsold certificates to a consortium of speculators for an undisclosed sum. He made only a little money.

Further Poyais schemes were equally successful. In 1828, MacGregor tried to sell land from Poyais at the price of 5 shillings per acre. In 1830, Robert Charles Frederic, brother and successor of King George Frederic, began to offer for sale the same territories to lumber companies. These certificates competed with those of MacGregor. When older investors demanded their interest, he could only pay with more certificates to the value of the interest payments he owed. Others began to use the same trick too – two men named Upton opened a rival "Poyaisian office" and offered land debentures for sale.

In 1831, MacGregor promoted a "Poyaisian New Three percent Consolidated Stock" as "the President of the Poyaisian Republic". In 1834, he was living in Scotland and had to issue a new series of land certificates as payment for unredeemed securities. In 1836, he wrote a new constitution for the Poyaisian Republic. The last record of any Poyais scheme is in 1837, when he tried to sell some land certificates.

In 1839, Gregor MacGregor moved to Venezuela where he had requested and received a pension as a general who had fought for independence. He died on December 4, 1845.

✿✿

The Ice King – Charles W. Morse

Charles Wyman Morse was a notorious businessman and speculator on Wall Street in the early 20th century.

Early life

Morse was born in Bath, Maine, in 1856, the son of Benjamin Wyman and Anna (Rodbird) Morse. His father had a large role in the towing business on the Kennebec River. Charles was already involved in the shipping business while a student at Bowdoin College, and at his graduation in 1877 he had accumulated a sizable capital. After college, he went into business with his father and a cousin, forming C.W. Morse & Company and engaging in an extensive business shipping ice and lumber.

On April 14, 1884, he married Hattie Bishop Hussey of Brooklyn, New York. She bore him three sons and a daughter, and died about 1897.

As his business interests grew, Morse moved to Boston and, in 1897, New York City.

The "Ice Trust"

He organised the Consolidated Ice Company in 1897 and went into the ice business. In 1899, he merged it with several other companies to form the American Ice Company which, grossly overcapitalised at $60 million, held a virtual monopoly for ice in New York. Morse quickly became known as "The Ice King".

On May 1, 1900, Morse attempted to use his monopoly to raise the price of ice. The plan backfired, however, and it was revealed by the *New York Journal and Advertiser* that Morse had obtained special privileges from Tammany Hall to run his business, and in exchange Robert Van Wyck (New York City's first mayor over the five united boroughs) had been given a substantial ownership share in the ice companies (by then known as the “Ice Trust”) as had Richard Croker, the boss of Tammany Hall. Having formed a holding company called the Ice Securities Company, Morse manipulated its stock and left the ice business with a profit of some $12 million.

Shipping and Banking

On June 18, 1901 he married Clemence Dodge, a divorcee from Atlanta, at the Fifth Avenue Presbyterian Church in Manhattan. The Morses lived at 724 Fifth Avenue, before moving to Lakewood Township, New Jersey. They maintained a summer home in Bath, Maine. Their marriage was annulled, however, in 1904 when it was determined that Clemence's divorce from her first husband, Charles F. Dodge, was not legal and she was therefore still married to him. Undeterred, she was represented by Samuel Untermyer, who restored her marital rights; she remained devotedly at the side of Morse until her death in 1926.

Morse returned to the realm of shipping in 1901 when he established the Eastern Steamship Company as a consolidation of three existing lines. These were the Boston and Bangor Steamship Company, dating from 1834; the Portland Steam Packet Company, organised in 1843; and the International Steamship Company, established in 1859.

In 1902, Morse acquired control of both overnight steamboat lines on the Hudson River – the People's Line, established in 1835, and the Citizens' Line, established in 1872 – and organised the Hudson Navigation Company to operate them. They were collectively known as the Hudson River Night Line. The People's Line named its new 411-foot steamer *C.W. Morse* in his honour in 1904. (Morse's uncle James Thomas Morse, his father's brother, was the namesake of the Rockland-Bar Harbour, Maine, steamer *J.T. Morse*, also built in 1904.)

Morse acquired control of the Metropolitan Steamship Company from the Whitney interests in 1906. He organised the Consolidated Steamship Company in January 1907 as a holding company for the Eastern Steamship Company, Metropolitan Steamship Company, Clyde Steamship Company and Mallory Steamship Company. Despite an initial announcement of such a sale, Morse failed in an attempt to purchase the Long Island Sound steamers of the New York, New Haven and Hartford Railroad. He did, however, acquire control of the New York and Cuba Mail Steamship Company and the New York and Porto Rico Steamship Company in 1907.

He parlayed this success into a prominent role in high finance in New York City. Morse controlled the National Bank of North America, the New Amsterdam National Bank and was a large owner of the Mercantile National Bank. He became a close associate of F. Augustus Heinze, who became president of Mercantile National, and E.R. Thomas, a young man of large inherited fortune. Their influence grew—Heinze and Morse served as directors together on at least six national banks, ten state banks, five trust companies and four insurance companies.

Panic of 1907

Along with Augustus Heinze's brothers, Morse helped create a pool of money to drive up and corner the stock of United Copper. On October 15, 1907 this corner failed so spectacularly that depositors with Morse's banks began to pull out their deposits. On October 20, the New York Clearing House, which had a critical role clearing cheques between banks, forced Morse to resign from his banking interests. This did not stop the panic, however, which went on to topple the Knickerbocker Trust

Company, New York's third largest trust, and led to financial turmoil across the country in November. The Morse-controlled steamship lines went into receivership, for varying periods, in February 1908.

Indicted by United States District Attorney Henry L. Stimson, Morse was convicted of violations of federal banking laws. He was sentenced to fifteen years in the Atlanta federal penitentiary in November 1908 but remained free on appeal.

On October 8, 1909, the assets of the Metropolitan Steamship Company were sold at foreclosure sale to John W. McKinnon of Chicago. The company was reincorporated three days later in Maine with Morse as president. The Metropolitan Steamship Company and Maine Steamship Company were consolidated with the Eastern Steamship Company in 1911 to form Eastern Steamship Corporation. This concern went into receivership in 1914 and emerged in 1917 as Eastern Steamship Lines.

Having exhausted his legal appeals, Morse departed for Atlanta penitentiary on January 2, 1910. In Atlanta, he was a prisoner alongside Charles Ponzi, who would go on to create an eponymous fraudulent financial scheme, the Ponzi scheme, and earn a legacy as one of the most famous swindlers in American history. Because of Morse's wealth and connections, he launched a campaign of lawyers, lobbyists and famous journalists like Clarence W. Barron who urged President William Howard Taft for leniency. In 1912 Morse became ill, and a panel of Army doctors declared that he suffered from Bright's disease and other maladies and would soon die if he remained in prison. Taft signed his pardon, and Morse departed for medical treatment at Wiesbaden. However, it soon became known to the Justice Department that he had feigned illness by drinking a combination of soapsuds and chemicals. Taft later said that the case "shakes one's faith in expert examination."

Later life and death

On his return from Europe, Morse returned to the shipping business. He still controlled the Hudson Navigation Company, which had not been involved in the crash of the Consolidated Steamship Company in 1907. Morse announced on January 11,

1916, plans for a new transoceanic steamship line, which he organised as the United States Shipping Company. This holding company exchanged its stock for that of sixteen subsidiary companies, each organised around a steamship.

During World War I, he organised the Virginia Shipbuilding Company and won contracts to build 36 vessels for the war effort. The freighters were ordered by the United States Shipping Board, and Morse borrowed from the Emergency Fleet Corporation funds to carry out the contracts. Ultimately, 22 of the ships were completed; the other 14 were cancelled.

Morse controlled the Hudson Navigation Company until its bankruptcy in 1921. The receivers quickly changed the name of the *C.W. Morse* to *Fort Orange*.

In 1922, Morse was accused of misrepresentation of his facilities for ship construction; misapplication of funds intended for the building of ships to the building of shipyards; misappropriation of equipment for his own purposes; and failure to turn over to the government the profits of ships it had leased to him. Indicted for war profiteering and fraud, soon after he was confronted with charges of mail fraud involving sales solicitations for stock of the United States Shipping Company. The trial on the war profiteering charges resulted in an acquittal, but a civil suit in 1925 against the Virginia Shipbuilding Company resulted in a judgment for the government of over $11.5 million. The mail fraud case against Morse ended when he was adjudged too ill to stand trial, and after a jury had disagreed the charges against his sons which were quashed.

His second wife, Clemence, died in July 1926. Suffering from paralysis, Morse was placed under the guardianship of the probate court of Bath on September 7, 1926, adjudged incompetent to handle his affairs. Having suffered several strokes, he died of pneumonia at Bath, Maine, on January 12, 1933.

✿✿

The French "Rockefeller"

Christophe Thierry Rocancourt, sometimes also called Christopher Rocancourt, (b. July 16, 1967 in Honfleur, France) is an impostor, confidence man and gentleman thief who scammed affluent people by masquerading as a French member of the Rockefeller family.

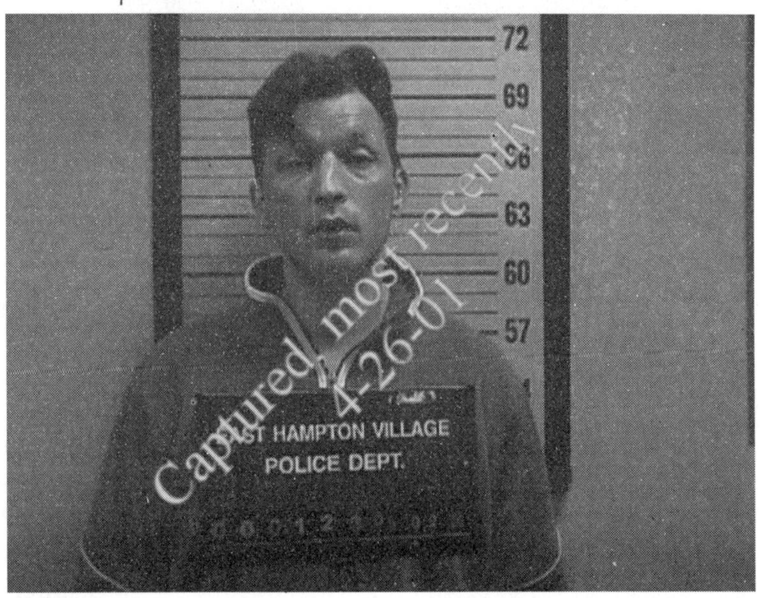

He told *Dateline NBC* in a 2006 broadcast that his mother sometimes worked as a prostitute and his father was an alcoholic who took Christopher to an orphanage when the boy was five. He ran away and made his way to Paris where he pulled his first big con: faking the deed to a property he didn't own, then "selling" the property for USD $1.4 million.

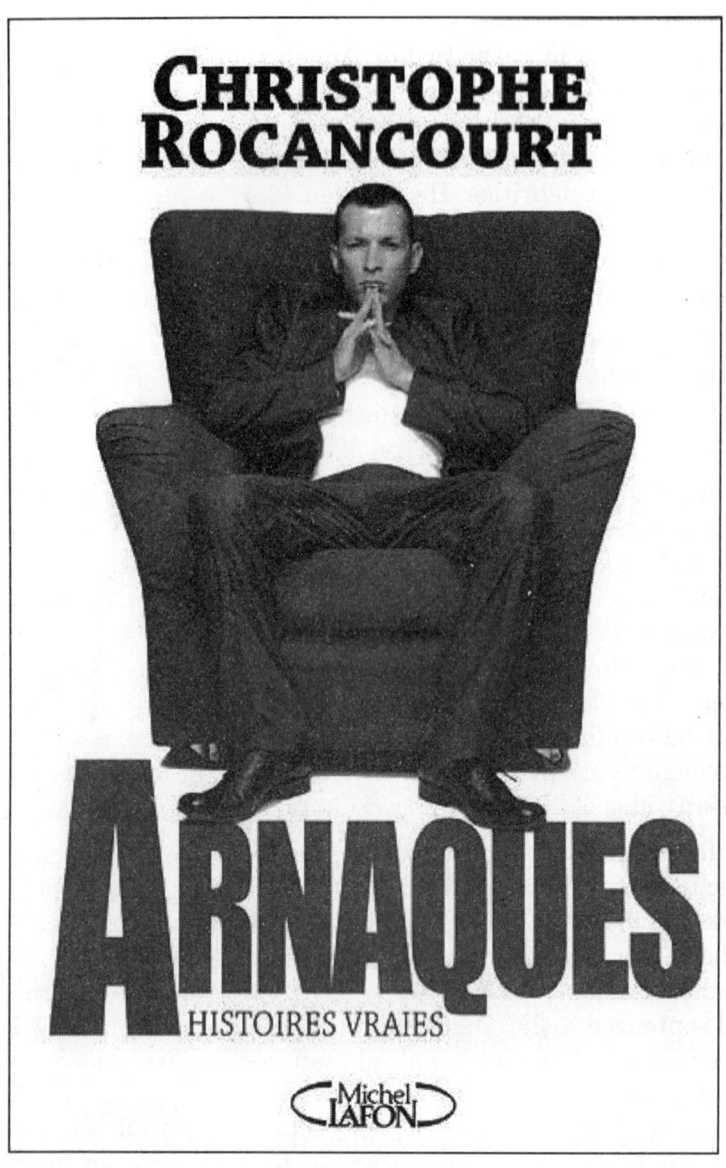

Making his way to the United States, Rocancourt used at least a dozen aliases. He got the rich and powerful to invest in his schemes, he told *Dateline*, by tapping into their greed. He convinced them that he, too, was rich by paying for their lavish dinners in cash. In Los Angeles, he pretended to be a movie producer, ex-boxing champion or venture capitalist. He dropped names like "his mother" Sophia Loren or "his uncles" Oscar de la Renta and Dino De Laurentiis and was associated with various celebrities. He married *Playboy* model Pia Reyes; they had a son, Zeus. He lived for a time with Mickey Rourke and apparently convinced actor Jean-Claude Van Damme to produce his next movie.

Beside being married to Pia Reyes, according to the press, he lived with playboy model Rhonda Rydell for six months. She did not know Rocancourt was married, and said he had told her he was French nobility, the son of a countess.

In 1997, police raided Rocancourt's hotel suite. In 1998, he was arrested for an involvement in a shootout and jumped bail. In 1999, he was freed of charges of forging passports after he had bribed State Department employees to get a passport. He was arrested in 2000 in the Hamptons for an unpaid hotel bill, then jumped bail. On April 27, 2001 he and Reyes were arrested in Oak Bay, British Columbia, Canada, and charged with defrauding an elderly couple. Reyes was released after convincing authorities that she had no part in the scam, much less any idea of her husband's criminal activities.

In Canada, Rocancourt wrote an autobiography in which he ridiculed his victims. In March 2002, he was extradited to New York and pleaded to charges of theft, grand larceny, smuggling, bribery, perjury and fraud against nineteen victims. He was fined $9 million, was ordered to pay $1.2 million in restitution and sentenced to five years in prison. In Switzerland, the police have connected him with a jewel theft and barred him from the country until 2016.

He once estimated to *Dateline* that his various schemes/ventures netted him at least $40 million (USD), but this cannot be confirmed. On June 7, 2006, the Associated Press reported that imprisoned former private investigator Anthony Pellicano performed an illegal background check on a law enforcement official who was investigating Rocancourt in a fake passport scheme.

In July 2009, French filmmaker Catherine Breillat accused Rocancourt of scamming her out of 850,000 Euros. Breillat, who was diagnosed with a cerebral vascular disease in 2004, said that "It's an abuse of weakness." Due to this event, the film "Bad Love", with Rocancourt and model Naomi Campbell, was cancelled. Breillat told a French journalist that her first meeting with Rocancourt was the worst day of her life, even worse than the day when she was diagnosed with her cerebral vascular disease.

✿✿

Rapidex Courses — Adopted by CRORES of readers

The largest selling sensation of all times

A course of just 60 days can make you speak English fluently and effortlessly, whatever be your mother tongue.

Published in sixteen languages

Hindi, Malayalam, Tamil, Telugu, Kannada, Marathi, Gujarati, Bangla, Oriya, Urdu, Assamese, Punjabi, Nepalese, Persian, Arabic and Sinhalese

th CD
D

....	Hindi	1226S	Assamese	1210S	Malayalam	1228S	Nepali		
....	Gujarati	1211S	Oriya	1209S	Tamil	1130B	Singhalese**		
....	Marathi	1203S	Punjabi	1204S	Telugu	1131C	Persian**		
....	Bangla	1205S	Kannada	1206S	Urdu	1127A	Arabic**		

Rapidex Dictionary of Spoken Words

98/- each

- 6611 G .... Eng.–Hindi
- 1133 A .... Eng.–Bangla
- 1132 D .... Eng.–Tamil
- 1134 B .... Eng.–Kannada
- 1136 D .... Eng.–Telugu
- 1137 A .... Eng.–Gujarati
- 1135 C .... Eng.–Malayalam

POPULAR SCIENCE

Save Rs.101/- Each Volume Rs.175/- Buy Complete Set (Four Volumes) for Rs. 599/-

Code: 4505 S — Set Code: 4510 S

- Four Volumes • Over 800 Pages
- Over 900 Illustrations • 890 Articles

Available in Hindi & English both

FREE CD

2214 S Rs. 120/- (Colour)

2213 S • Rs. 120/- (Colour)

Rs. 180/-

6679 A • Rs. 150/-

6647 F • Rs. 450/- (HB)

9412 C • Rs. 96/-

A 12-Volume series teaching 6 Regional Languages through Hindi & vice versa

132/- each

1218S	Hindi-Bangla	1214S	Hindi-Malayalam
1224S	Bangla-Hindi	1220S	Malayalam-Hindi
1219S	Hindi-Gujarati	1215S	Hindi-Tamll
1225S	Gujarati-Hindi	1221S	Tamil-Hindi
1216S	Hindi-Kannada	1217S	Hindi-Telugu
1222S	Kannada-Hindi	1223S	Telugu-Hindi

PERSONS & PERSONALITIES

Rs. 150/-

5178 E • Rs. 72/-

8991 D • Rs. 120/-

5122 L • Rs. 72/-

51102 • Rs. 72/-

4176 B • Rs. 395/- (H.B.)

195/- with CD

1112S ....

295/- with CD

1234S ....

PERSONALITY DEVELOPMENT

9450 B • Rs. 195/-

5642 A • Rs. 150/-

9447 C • Rs. 88/-
8966 E • Rs. 88/-

9973 E • Rs. 110/-

5639 B • Rs. 75/-

9070 B • Rs. 175/-

8868 D • Rs. 150/-

9028 D • Rs. 120/-

9981 B • Rs. 120/-

9088 C • Rs. 195/-

8997 B • Rs. 96/-

9430 B • Rs.150/-

COMPUTERS

0000 • Rs. 150/- 7766 A • Rs. 120/- 946

7712 K • Rs. 96/- 7711 J • R

PARENTING

8261 D • Rs. 150/-

8919 D • R

SAYINGS/QUOTATI PROVERBS

8963 B • Rs. 80/- 9953 A •

8999 D • Rs. 80/- 5512 A •

9346 C • Rs. 60/- 9425 A •

STUDENT DEVELOPMENT

9457 E • Rs. 150/-

9455 C • Rs. 150/-

8962 A • Rs. 96/-

4016 D • Rs. 96/-

9089 D • Rs. 135/-

9967 C • Rs. 120/-

9071 D • Rs. 96/-

2244 D • Rs. 60/- H

9441 S • Rs. 195/-

5622 A • Rs. 108/-

9090 A • Rs. 160/-

2241 J • Rs. 68/-

BODY/BEAUTY CARE

8093 D • Rs. 150/-

9986 B • Rs. 120/-

9922 F • Rs. 96/-

8865 F • Rs. 90/-

8971 B • Rs. 96/-

LOVE, SEX & ROMANCE

8260 D • Rs. 96/-

8266 D • Rs. 80/-

8278 C • Rs. 80/-

8916 D • Rs. 68/-

8268 C • Rs. 175/-

SELF-IMPROVEMENT

Rs. 195/- | 9096 B • Rs. 96/- | 4008 J • Rs. 96/- Ⓑ | 9027 D • Rs. 120- | 8258 D • Rs. 120/- | 9026 D • Rs. 175/- | 9563 N • Rs. 125/-

Rs. 80/- | 9066 B • Rs. 96/- | 9081 D • Rs. 96/- | 4010 L • Rs. 60/- | 9091 B • Rs. 80/- | 8885 D • Rs. 68/- | 8947 E • Rs. 80/-

Rs. 96/- | 8943 C • Rs. 195/- | 8935 D • Rs. 96/- | 8990 C • Rs. 96/-

JOB / CAREER

5623 B • Rs. 195/- | 9404 D • Rs. 195/-

9439 C • Rs. 150/- | 9431 C • Rs.175/-

4017 D • Rs. 120/- | 4018 D • Rs. 80/- | 9535 C • Rs. 150/-

DIET & NUTRITION

Rs. 96/- | 8985 B • Rs. 69/- | 8904 D • Rs. 96/- | 8276 A • Rs. 80/- | 8968 G • Rs. 96/-

RELATIONSHIP

G • Rs. 72/- | 8998 C • Rs. 80/- | 9438 B • Rs.150/- | 9065 A • Rs. 80/- | 9994 E • Rs. 120/-

ALTERNATIVE THERAPIES

8983 E • Rs. 80/- | 8941 A • Rs. 80/- | 8879 C • Rs. 60/- | 5637 D • Rs. 96/-

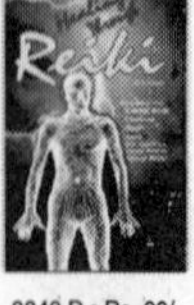

8882 F • Rs. 150/- | 8842 D • Rs. 80/- | 8889 D • Rs. 80/- | 8836 D • Rs. 135/-

8271 C • Rs. 96/- | 2317 E • Rs. 60/- | 9935 F • Rs. 108/- | 9950 B • Rs. 80/-

GENERAL HEALTH

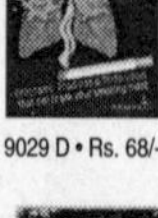
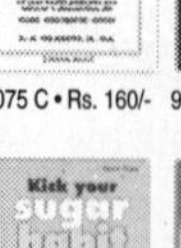

8877 A • Rs. 120/- | 8870 D • Rs. 60/- | 9029 D • Rs. 68/- | 9075 C • Rs. 160/- | 9940 D • Rs. 120/-

8938 D • Rs. 88/- | 8948 A • Rs. 96/- | 9025 D • Rs. 80/- | 9038 D • Rs. 68/- | 8859 G • Rs. 80/-

SLIMMING & FITNESS

9445 A • Rs. 150/- | 8277 B • Rs. 80/- | 8875 K • Rs. 80/- | 8847 M • Rs. 60/-

COMMON AILMENTS & DISEASES

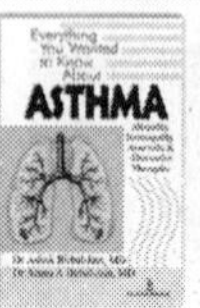

8281 A • Rs. 80/- | 8094 D • Rs. 120/- | 8888 D • Rs. 80/- | 8908 D

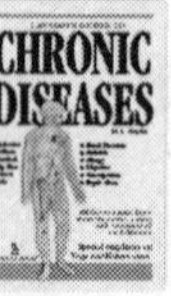
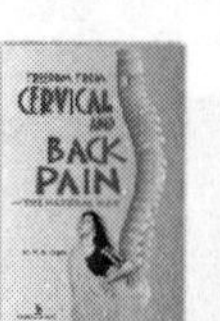
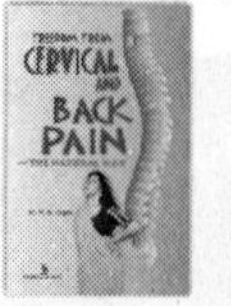

8964 C • Rs. 96/- | 8848 D • Rs. 96/- | 8878 B • Rs. 80/- | 8891 D

YOGA & MEDITATION

2118 F • Rs.120/- | 8269 A • Rs.150/- | 9087 B • Rs.96/- | 9998 D •

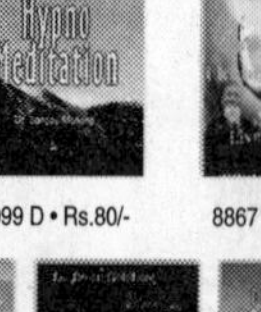

9080 C • Rs.24/- | 8939 D • Rs.88/- | 8099 D • Rs.80/- | 8867 D

8901 D • Rs.120/- | 9958 S • Rs.160/- (with CD) | 2119 G • Rs.96/- | 8892 D • Rs.120/- | 9057

HOMEOPATHY

9446 B • Rs.150/- | 8887 D • Rs.175/- | 8270 B •

3 A • Rs.340/- HB

4128 D • Rs. 250/- Colour (H.B.)

4177 C • Rs. 295/- (H.B.)

9987 E • Rs. 150/-

9585 A • Rs. 96/-

9983 D • Rs. 499/- Colour (H.B.)

3 D • Rs.95/-

4126 B • Rs. 96/-

9505 A • Rs.195/-

4183 A • Rs. 350/- (H.B.)

9514 B • Rs.60/-

4151 A • Rs. 399/- Colour (H.B.)

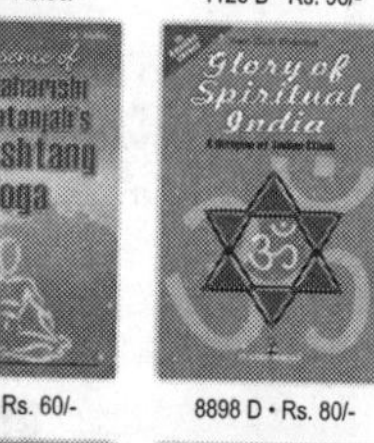
3 A • Rs. 60/-

8898 D • Rs. 80/-

4124 A • Rs. 80/-

9405 A • Rs. 195/-

4190 C • Rs. 160/-

9984 E • Rs. 399/- Colour (H.B.)

A • Rs.175/-

9520 D • Rs. 120/-

9510 B • Rs.120/-

9542 B • Rs. 150/-

4182 D • Rs. 96/-

4130 B • Rs. 120/-

4152 B • Rs. 96/-

• Rs. 80/-

9509 A • Rs.150/-

9407 C • Rs. 195/-

9525 A • Rs. 150/-

9504 D • Rs.96/-

9989 D • Rs. 96/-

4181 C • Rs. 195/-

9540 D • Rs. 150/-

A • Rs. 80/-

4179 A • Rs. 295/- (H.B.)

4132 D • Rs. 80/-

9063 D • Rs. 80/-

9997 C • Rs. 80/-

Commenteries on BHAGAVAD GITA

9959 D • Rs. 80/- 4113 D • Rs. 48/- 4188 A • Rs. 160/-

COOKERY BOOKS

9936 D • Rs. 96/- 9320 A • Rs. 125/- 9297 C • Rs. 125/- 9948 D • Rs. 80/- 9938 D • Rs. 80/-

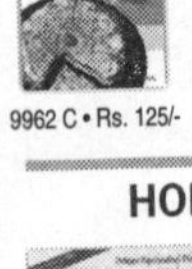

9962 C • Rs. 125/- 9942 D • Rs. 80/- 9944 D • Rs. 80/- 9943 D • Rs. 80/-

HOMEMAKING / GRILLS & RAILINGS

3111 E • Rs. 175/- 3107 F • Rs. 88/- 3106 E • Rs. 88/- 3108 G • Rs. 90/-

3102 K • Rs. 195/- (H.B.) 3103 L • Rs. 88/- 3104 M • Rs. 88/- 3105 D • Rs. 88/-

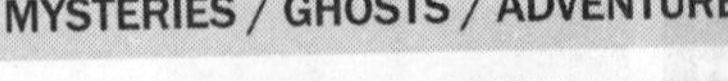

MYSTERIES / GHOSTS / ADVENTURE

2331 C • Rs. 60/- 2335 A • Rs. 80/- 9985 A • Rs. 80/- 5164 E • R

9977 B • Rs. 96/- 2337 C • Rs. 96/- 2336 B • Rs. 80/- 51107 • R

5156 D • Rs. 72/- 5172 F • Rs. 72/- 5121 K • Rs. 72/- 5116 D •

JOKES

2319 B • Rs. 96/- 2341 B • Rs. 60/- 2318 A • Rs. 80/- 2330 B • Rs. 80/- 9226 A

HUMOUR & SATIRE

2338 D • Rs. 120/- 8890 D • Rs. 68/- 2315 C • Rs. 80/- 2321 D • Rs. 295/- (H.B.) 9340 A • Rs. 96/- 8927 D • Rs. 68/- 2326 E • Rs. 120/-

QUIZ BOOKS

8965 D • Rs. 96/- 7727 L • Rs. 72/- 7723 F • Rs. 72/- 7726 K • Rs. 72/- 7753 G • Rs. 72/- 7722 E • Rs. 72/- 7725 J • Rs. 72/-

Moral, Wisdon Fairy Tales

TALES OF WISDOM

8967 F • Rs. 96/- 9077 E • R

9248 C • Rs. 60/- 2289 D • R

ASTROLOGY / VASTU / HYPNOTISM / PALMISTRY

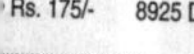
• Rs. 175/-

8925 D • Rs. 80/-

8899 D • Rs. 110/-

9432 D • Rs.150/-

8259 D • Rs. 88/-

2125 D • Rs. 80/-

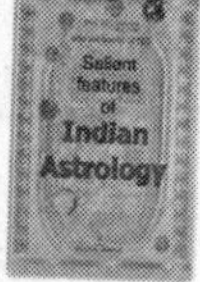

2133 B • Rs. 96/-

2109 F • Rs. 120/-

8902 D • Rs. 80/-

• Rs. 150/-

2127 D • Rs. 150/-

9086 A • Rs. 295/- (HB)

2112 D • Rs. 80/-

2108 E • Rs. 80/-

2116 D • Rs. 110/-

3110 D • Rs. 96/-

2120 D • Rs. 96/-

ENGLISH IMPROVEMENT

• Rs. 175/-

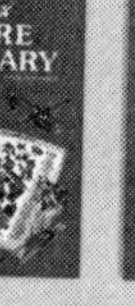

5511 E • Rs. 72/-

6651 E • Rs. 175/-

5538 D • Rs. 80/-

6607 L • Rs. 88/-

5541 C • Rs. 196/-

9040 D • Rs. 60/-

9056 A • Rs. 96/-

GENERAL

. 80/-HB

9041 A • Rs.195/-

5114 B • Rs.68/-

4175 A • Rs. 195/-

9532 D • Rs. 250/- HB

MAGIC

2250 A • Rs. 110/-

2202 E • Rs. 80/-

2237 M • Rs. 60/-

2242 K • Rs. 60/-

2243 L • Rs. 60/-

FUN, FACTS

60/-

9326 B • Rs. 96/-

6690 D • Rs. 60/-

2328 G • Rs. 50/-

2327 F • Rs. 50/-

2211 F • Rs. 60/-

5110 A • Rs. 80/-

MANAGEMENT / BUSINESS & PROFESSION / STOCK MARKET

9461 K • Rs. 135/-

5638 A • Rs. 110/-

8979 A • Rs. 96/-

9406 B • Rs. 150/-

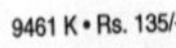

5646 A • Rs. 225/-

5643 B • Rs. 120/-

8972 C • Rs. 80/-

9402 B • Rs. 195/-

5614 E • Rs. 150/-

9079 B • Rs. 195/-

9403 C • Rs. 195/-

5618 D • Rs. 88/-

5615 D • Rs. 150/-

4001 A • Rs. 150/-

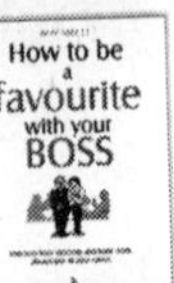

4004 D • Rs. 88/-

5641 D • Rs. 195/- (H.B.)

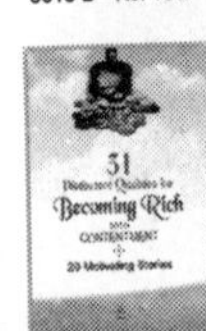

5640 C • Rs. 120/-

9313 D • Rs. 150/-

8883 D • Rs. 120/-

4005 E • Rs. 96/-

AYURVEDA

8923 D • Rs. 150/-

8010 D • Rs. 88/-

8944 D • Rs. 175/-

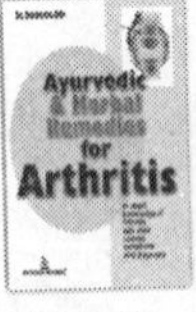
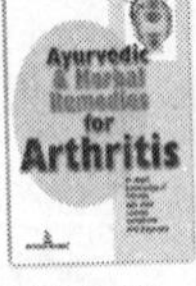

9094 E • Rs. 96/-

FICTION from Cedar books

9459 H • Rs. 1000/-

9587 C • Rs. 125/-

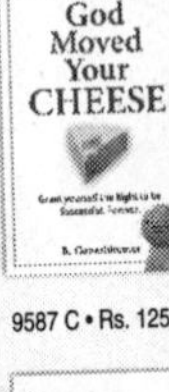

9582 T • Rs. 150/-

9532 D • Rs.

9526 B • Rs. 125/-

9592 H • Rs. 150/-

9512 D • Rs. 250/-

9501 A •

9530 B • Rs. 175/-

9560 J • Rs. 175/-

9544 D • Rs. 95/-

9522B •

Title	Price
Fate, Fraud & A Friday Wedding	150.00
The Ultimate Laugh	150.00
Cricket Till I Die!	150.00
Delayed Mansoon	150.00
What Happened to That Love	125.00
Did you see The Joker?	125.00
Luv U Mate	125.00
Kalika	175.00
Love was never Mine	150.00
The K-Word	150.00
Temple of Destiny	175.00
The Adventure of the Bubblegum Boy	150.00
Truly, Madly, Deeply	175.00
The Long Road	150.00
The Unheards	150.00
To catch a Butterfly	95.00
It can't be you...	175.00
Far From Normal	150.00
Somewhere@nowhere	150.00
Deceivers	150.00
Some of the Whole	199.00
Love on Velocity Express	125.00
A River on fire	95.00
A Nameless Place	125.00
Incredible High	175.00
One Day	125.00

- Fallen Leaf, Withered Wind
- Foot Print in The Bajra
- Haunting Silhouettes
- How I got my Girl Back
- Interpretation
- The Red Corridor
- The God who failed!
- Prisoners of Hate
- The Wheel Turned
- Beyond Diamond Rings
- Mask in the Mirror
- Dance O' Peacock
- Enemy in the Ranks
- Friendship@ facebook.com
- Vinculum
- Dancing on the notes of life
- Illusions of Love
- Kite Strings
- Knots and No Crosses
- Men as they are!
- Not for $ Anymore
- Three Shades of Green
- The Angel of God
- The Journey of Om
- The Second Hand
- Under the rain tree